MW00778845

Free-spirited Poems

Bodies & souls speak a volume

Rodney Richards

IMPORTANT

Trade print ISBN 979-8990453616

Library of Congress Control Number: 2024921415

eBook ISBN 979-8990453623

Cover by Jesse Richards, author/artist of *Unknown New York* et al. https://www.jesserichards.com/shelf/

First edition

Published by ABLiA Media LLC, Hamilton NJ USA

Disclaimers

Contents

Death

Playful

FUD & FUBAR walk into a bar

Arrogance of Seagulls by Marion Pollack

monetized eyeballs

what nice mounds you have...

Yes, Virginia, lead still exists

I swear

won million-dollar jackpot

The Language of Cancer

water runs

Ellen's Underwear*

decisions decisions

Loss of love

Boyhood inheritance

If not happy now...

Among the Wild by Patricia LeBon Herb

Muse for a Poem

His *Hallo!* cures the world's woes

a foreign car

robbed at McDonald's

Americanisms

If I had your AK-47

America's couple

Treasury Tower

americans run

Marketing 101

animal restaurants

Night Sledding by Donald Proffit

Conundrum

death shucks over 50 bucks

Silent light, Holy light

There once was a man from Hershey

The Most Great War

be proud

Big Red's Legacy

I am not a cook

How you's doin'?

horsedrawn carriages

Surreal and real

I Hear Voices

In-A-God-finda-Da-Vida

Songs of Earth

Blowing

Waking and Dreaming

if i don't change

Undying Fire

Ego Dictionary

Meditation 1

Meditation 2

Meditation 3

Meditation 4

FutureVision

Undying Fire II

Daily living

Black hat riders

fun on a summer day by elliot m rubin

Love Thomas'

The Lawnmower

Yardville Park Solitude

Credo of Grandpa by Michael P. Riccards, PhD

Beware WYSIWYG

Where's the Maytag repairman?

Recycle if you care

The man of action*

surf city by Joan Menapace

Battlefield love

Stopped counting anniversaries

we all stop here

say something

daily news on hiatus

don't write much

Rocking the world

Age of Aquarius

Cream

if I leave her alone

Rock It Twice

Give it Time

drivin' the danger highway

Modern History Lessons

why don't i ask

praise be to the brave

Eternity

Give me thangs like James Brown

Psychedelic music

I'm not old

strange new language brew

Pandora will release it again

What futures hold

Bachelor

The Other by Craig Sherman

Ghost lover's voice

better to say...

here... take it

heart sighs a breath by William Waldorf

what's pinochle among friends

Another day better than good

On Writing

on my gravestone

every poet writes a love poem

dozens a day

Three

Write Anything

Kill

Selfish love

Blood ink

Sonnrick I: To writers*

organic menthol

_Toc1796 Error! Bookmark not defined.

Apolitical

can't escape

blessed with two

MIA again

don't judge a book

I call them to account

Jabbingwhackies*

Some can't forgive

Free speech hijacked

each vote gold lamé

Another white rich demagogue

To

Women of the World—brilliant, funny, smart, caring, long-suffering, loving, patient and free-spirited beyond description.

Mom, in her nineties. My biggest fan. Still sharp and beats me at Skip-Bo.

Janet, my teenage love, helpmate, supporter, cheerleader, caregiver, muse and faithful partner in all the worlds of God.

Kate, our talented, level-headed daughter and Rocking Candles solopreneur, and Rachel, our daughter-in-law, two-time author, renowned massage therapist, singer and actress. Both excellent mothers.

and would-be poets

No matter your type, origin or background, sex, class, creed, nationality, tribe, orientation, or color, you are a human, and every human is a poet.

Let your poet soar. Make a start. Transcribe your inspirations long or short. Surprise us. Write, edit, and polish until stopping. Then publish, because you must publish, so that the world hears you. Become a Diamond album singer/artist with dulcet tones.

Poems are never final.

They are free spirits like you.

Good ones live on.

Just like you.

Short intro

I was born in our nation's capital the same May Day that Mosinee, Wisconsin renamed itself Moskva in a mock communist takeover of the town. Scary world then; scarier now.

Hospitalized after a manic episode at age 29, mood stabilizers and anti-psychotics pills keep me "normal."

Locked inside my first clinic, I read a beat-up volume of
Edgar Allan Poe's complete works, swooning over his emotive
power. I am a logophile, logos and philos melded together.

My attempts in my later writings to capture a moment or
impression like Poe did, are inadequate I admit. I can't do justice
to the infinite, or to a robin, pine tree, rosebush, raven at the door,
or Google's new AI brain. We process the infinite our own way.

I do believe our unique and eternal Rational Soul provides the
major tool to set free our potentialities. Time, by seconds or
decades, and events, tiny or huge, is necessary also.

I'm merely an observer and cub reporter, a budding essayist
and expressionist, describing what I experience, think, know or
feel. Who I am and words, to me, stay the same on every page.
Like truth, they are immortal. At the same time, they change to
keep up with changing times. The sole constant in creation is
change. That is soul.

My American Jimmy Olsen doesn't grab headlines, or always
say it right, or get natural laughs. I'm not witty like my son Jesse.
I apologize if something offends you. Poetry is subjective, seen
and felt through the poet's eyes, ears, pen, fingertips, body,
experiences, emotions, hopes, dreams and the unknowable. But
not the unthinkable.

I realize few things exist as either 100% this or that. There are
extremes, outliers, exceptions, differences, unknowns and the
unforeseen, even ignorance. So please take generalities as
general.

However, believe that each of us has stories and poems in us.
Let them roar.

I've added a few notes in places for context, and I thank my
personal friends and poets for their contributions.

Women and men

A million times more than males ascribe to them as objects, overall mistreatment of women is well documented. Until men control their urges and alter their views, women will remain suppressed. The equality of men and women will be achieved when men promote and champion it.

Persian sage and spiritual religious leader 'Abdu'l-Bahá said, "...women go neck and neck with the men. In no movement will they be left behind. Their rights with men are equal in degree.... They will attain in all such a degree as will be considered the very highest station of the world of humanity and will take part in all affairs. Rest ye assured. Do ye not look upon the present conditions; in the not far distant future the world of women will become all-refulgent and all-glorious....

"...the entrance of women into all human departments is an irrefutable and incontrovertible question. No soul can retard or prevent it."—*Paris Talks*, p. 182

"Am I good enough? Yes, I am."—Michelle Obama, *Becoming,* writer, lawyer, first African-American First Lady of the United States, 2009-2017.

"Women have always been the strong ones of the world."—Coco Chanel, founder and namesake of the Chanel brand, credited in the post-World War I era with popularizing sporty, casual chic as the feminine standard of style.

"It took me quite a long time to develop a voice, and now that I have it, I am not going to be silent."—Madeleine Albright, American diplomat and political scientist who served as the 64th U.S. secretary of state.

"Some leaders are born women."—Geraldine Ferraro, Italian-American politician, diplomat, and attorney. A Democratic Party nominee for vice president in the 1984 presidential election and U.S. Representative from 1979 to 1985.

don't worry, be happy

played Marley's accapella reggae to
students in spiritual uplift café
wife's idea of course, not mine

She's so lively, positive, gay strangers
say, feel like close-knit brothers sisters
unlike dull as cardboard husband

Why'd she choose me? a senior at 18
when crossed the wood gym floor at
high school dance, brazen smile open
inviting, took my nervous clammy hand

swallowing shyness, walked red to car door
Liverpool four had shouted last refrains
I Wanna Hold Your Hand, shy lips
kissed her cheek, a junior teenage impulse

her red hair, freckles, twinkling eyes
captured my heart throbs within two weeks
locked schedules, became a permanent couple
unknown how though *why on Earth?*

where does her love come from these
fifty years wed in the same abode, Archangel
Gabriel knows she makes me feel forever
tied, heartstrings still sing that British song
I wanna be your man

Through

In the bright sun, gawd,
she brightens dull existences
Grace Kelly returns

Laughing After by Sash Kalansuriya

My little girl that dances,
How the world it seemed back then
To fail again
When now it hardly seems failing at all.
How I saw you vaguely through the window,
Through the backs of many frayed coats
Phrased in browns and grey.
It was for you I came
To watch you dance behind the counter
In that little store by the sea.
Years beyond my wisdom
When I knew not where to keep my hands
You held them there in yours.
Thinking now,
Sitting by you,
The way words live
In warm thoughts and whispers of our elders,
How 'All these years later
Still she checks her face
Before she goes to see him.'
May it be like this always.

Naani Love

hello there sweet sexy
thing in skintight jeans
ouch! you didn't have to slap me
because of my thoughts!

Haiku love

Sweetheart, I slapped you
for not asking me my name
I'm not your plaything!

Comparisons

no facsimile, nor as, nor like, nor synonym
no metaphor, nor clichéd yesterdays or today's bon mois
available to human mind, tongue, heart, fingers, speech
in whatever era, age, culture tribe or history book
explains prescient gifts endowed on earthly women
deploringly, poorly, wrongfully, woefully judged inferior
by pinprick pinhole pindick male comprehension.
put right hand on Bible and swear its true

Women

What dare I reply
when text *you want me to die*
My heart breaks for you

if they're worth it

don't fret if some jerk says
you misunderstood
try it again, once more, again I say
no time for recriminations

words can be changed
hurts drowned or forgotten
social conduct fall into disfavor
I know you'll get it right

if you hear me say *i'm sorry*
you can't read minds, not yet
you feel what you think i mean
i will always love you

people don't say blank enough

Glad we live together
Such a terrific companion
Makes me bust a laugh
You're a funny, vibrant girl
So happy

letter to mom on her 91st birthday

put on your reading glasses
pop in your Miracle Ears
listen to these words so hard to tell you
it's heavy being first born of five
overly embarrassed from hugs and kisses
but feel them.. hidden.. respond inside

like Norma Jean you stunned your young beaus
after honeymoon uncovered how Dad two-timed you
single, raised us boys on your own, with three more
until Catholic hospital doctor whispered in your ear.
I knew, didn't want to break the news, upset you
when your second died of AIDS at thirty-five—
you didn't tell me until ten years later

us siblings chipped in when you 83, we jetted
across windy Atlantic sharing past loves and deprivations
visited your emerald homeland and drank back Jameson.
packing your suitcase to leave I said
a sheep wool sweater too bulky, will not fit.
crushed your spirit *it's heavy being your first love child*
regret not giving you the one thing you wanted most
what you hoped that first wedding day from
the love who broke your heart for bachelor sex—
a contented Catholic church-going family

Sigh

Horrible. her face downcast, visibly shaken
my best first wife turns her face aside
   signals no more subtle interrogation
could never bring myself to ask details
no matter how relaxed her expression
   Don't want to remind her… of my secret episode
across the Atlantic, London, Rome, overhead Turkey
   told no one I left, still too upsetting.
ironic when tell visitors, family, guests
   Let me tell ya; the Basilica's mammoth, but
don't add, *Tried to climb to the top of its dome* or
when stood, unzipped, pissed in middle of a Tel Aviv street or
smoked Marlboros while stuck at Athens airport as
   men with Uzis debated passport next step

not concerned over mental illness
or pity myself a foolish sufferer
   not that trip nor two, or three thereafter
society's unfair label denigrates disease, not me
another Wikipedia list mental incapacity
   while hundreds run rampant in America.
must take meds daily, second nature
carry pill case when out of town
   safer… I guess… *Sigh* exits throat
she waits. Anxious
at the door for my return
   bless her undying faith

If Selma were a woman

Left movie theatre
in tears. Deep south prejudice.
Cradled head in arms

A Work in Progress by TARA

Tell me no tale so I'll tell you no lie
Hear my honesty deafen my cry
Everything is not something we long to try

Helpless not hopeless; yes I still fly
Undone not broken; I will defy
Ruined; not shameless so why am I shy

I tell you no secrets but catch truths in my eye
Search for its meaning even though I am sly

Tears fall and tumble but with joy may I die
Oppression over and done with
I'll let haters pass by

Virtual reality like the blue of my sky
Experience euphoria; I'll escape in the high
Rejoice for a moment for I do and don't; won't die

crimes against life

do not force me to recount rape onslaughts
I cannot grant forgiveness to perpetrators
no impulse, motive, reason, insanity
jealousy, justification nor any excuse is valid
happy you're caught, your warped body
now clasps thick unbreakable iron-cold bars
your only weekday visitors
solitary confinement
your only weeknight visitors
devils of lost freedoms

face it brothers

women suns stars planets moons, not statues
    men the marble gods of Roman centurions
hail from the galaxy's darkest reddest planet.
    women born of Mother Gaia, Venus
men devilish hellhound demons, Ares their commander
    fleshly sorrows of weak humans invoke their mirth.
women angels, patient, marry us when proposed
    touch our cold hearts with salt-dried tears
in love and cherishment, perform every asked task.
    we respond in spades not hearts, lie, cheat, seal our lips
escape to bars or potato couches, let you raise kids
    on your own, dish out beatings when home

soldier-citizen mercenaries we men all go to war
    shoot for sport, exult in esprit de corps.
women nurse injured, bury innocent newborns.
    but if we're strong, we try to break harsh male molds
stereotypes of rotten fathers, *boys must be men* and so on
    eschew *do not cry or frown,* melt our ice cube hearts.
We would change if didn't fear derision
    live in your dresses, bras, flats, panties, high heel shoes
learn empathy besides wanting to get laid.
    as kind brothers who banish stone hearts, rough tones
no longer remote, no longer lifeless dead asteroids
    we wouldn't die bereft, needlessly marooned

A goddess

Her black bikini
jumped my tan 15 year bones
to her 22

Husband off to war
to naïve or scared for what
she wanted that day

Facing East by Jonathan Savrin

The sphere of yellow light pierced the black cloudless horizon

Heat transformed the dew into a mist hovering above the grassland.

Baby robins were roused

     in their snug nest and opened

     their mouths skyward chirping for food.

A hawk searched

     for thermals in the rising temperature to lift

     him in a circular path to new heights.

An old man inhaled the still crisp air deep into his lungs,

     reviving his soul with gratitude for the gift of

     daily rebirth

The young lovers entangled in an undulating embrace,

     wondered what adventures and gifts awaited them

     this new day

for a brave spouse

glad for her three weak smiles today
to match total lack of muscle strength
numbing pains in calves, feet
makes her face ornery sour

crush pills into Mott's applesauce
only way she swallows if not liquid
crush pills first, then split black/white capsule
for little extended-release relief
suck up liquid pain killer into syringe
says stop at 10 milliliters (for good luck?)
she downs tiny sips, drools through two napkins
timed routines routine these past two months
since cancer ravaged blue-thin veiny blood
It's on fire, neurologist director said
no reaction from her. my stomach lurches

each morn demands Ensure or coconut water,
throat nerves sting like daggers, tongue shrunken cadaver
may feel cool surcease from coffee ice cream taste
speaks in garbled mumbles, moans, low groans
sounds hard to interpret, fail more often, thumbs up *yes*
angry, she scribbles hieroglyphics on white napkins
makes me feel her demand, command, plea, cry
decimate half a bag of Bounty thick ones weekly

she repeats *I'm dying* without remorse
somehow strong enough to survive another day
as get to bed after *Wheel,* lay next to her, supine
blurred eyes beg God's blessings, I cry inside
as her tears of frustration hit water-filled pillow.
caregiver no longer; fulltime caretaker my 24/7 role
can only make her IKEA graveside bed
more comfortable as time together ends

no good way to say this...

only 6:10   plenty of time   before cancer day train arrives
when she wakes must pour liquid meds
    PEG plastic yellow tube in her stomach awaits.
have a quick smoke   rush to Dunkin' for joe
    in line, miffed at SUV ahead   large order takin' time
    ponder his *Praise the Lord* red bumper sticker
slow to pull away, the jerk, doesn't care   my turn at last
on drive home sip hot fresh coffee   revives
    notice 7:32 on dash
Oh no   Daylight Saving Time   late, she must be awake
    hit the gas...pull in...park...enter house...push door
no light, not sittin' there fumin', irate   sigh relief
    I'll check at 8   she'll be ready for sure
look up from typin' political haibun   10 after
    where is she? So prompt, a Swiss clock
    should have heard her walker scrape wood floor
climb basement steps to see   knock   push door further
    spy queen-size foam bed   *loves her privacy*
    a solitude fortress since last year's diagnosis
tiptoe down hall on soft carpet threads
    lies on her left side   quiet, petite
extremely unlike her   inch closer, check, 20 past...
    hon, hon?
no response
    a breath   pause   brush her ear   *Hon?*
not a stir   louder   *HON?*
    eerie silence   scream   *H O N!*
drop down   grab her hip   shake   not a stir
    try again   not a movement, not a whimper
turn her back flat   she dreams   eyelids shut
    no dry spittle on her open mouth
    like my brother
press her wrist...limp...fish out of water
    crap, crap, crap
    ...oh honey

Purrfect together

You're a purrfect New Jersey girl
    befits Aphrodite's sculpted face
    under flaming red curls
Countenance of beauty, strength, intelligence, grace

Lips roam over smooth salt-sweat neck
    Slow, methodical, toward heaven below
Slight curves of downy-haired skin
    allure grows   reach small of back
flow of pale upraised hip

Fingers dance
    squeeze firm compliant buttocks
    hands outstretched
Energy rises upon young golden thigh
    thy long leg beckons

Hand flitters on mounding calf
    returns to inner thigh
Raise smooth-skinned leg
    akimbo… pause

Upon thy virgin flesh
    familiar to my touch
    move nearer…
Closer to moist expectation

Aroused, hard, push
    stretch to reach thy length
    matching mine
Fingers gently probe
    through thy curly bush
to promised mutual release

    Soft, soft, keep it soft
    though difficult to brake
    walk fingertips along skin lightly

A rush, a brush, more touch,
    thy secretest self exposed
moans escape inflamed mouth

Senses occupied, smells of heat escape
Tastes and images of
    imminent joy
Whilst another, drawn-out groan
    betrays tongue's
penetrating passions

Hips grind once…twice…in rhythm
    responsive to thumb's pushes
bare vulva projection reached
    then gently… pull away

Up flat tummy to
    even firmer breast once more
    press hard areola's breast
between thumb, forefinger's test
    ready

Left hand palm
    grasps thy shivering
thighs, force downward gently

Now flat, susceptible
    same as I
Whilst spirit's truth whispers --
    palms lift my frame
above thine own, supine

Expectations higher than
    anticipation's taste of surrender
imagine our lovemaking
    as remember us on this bed
twenty years ago

'Twas Beauty killed the beast

impresario Carl Denham said, sad when
Kong toppled off the city's Empire peak in '33
leaving blonde Ann Darrow on brick-made balcony
but was a pixie redhead with freckles toppled me
when said, *Tell me about yourself*

saw Charlize in her then, saw my sob-filled beauty
cry out her love words *Oh, Joe!* to the
15-foot-tall Mighty Mister Young in '98
better FX than original Kong by far
Ebert gave it high score

I heaved, held breath at such luscious beauty
her silk white gown draped on dance floor
glowing deep bronze skin under curly blonde hair.
More alluring than Fay's demurity

apologize, apologize, my urges still part beast
movie maven maidens inflame this body's arteries
when real life babes surprise this old untamed lion
like Bo's 10, Hepburn's haughtiness, Tron's Olivia.
Starlets enamor, but marry their kind
uncontrollable lust unrequited in Hollywood
Redhead lover said it best
As if you stood a chance

Thank you

So inadequate
Ten times more inadequate
mere thank you's express

steadfastness

I want to stay married.
    We'll see, she says.
she's administered care to kids and me
together our story half written in
life's hurts, needs, slights of mistaken love.
melodramatic truth finds expression

when mania sprouts, or anger
need steadfast biblical savior
like she when says, *Hold it together*

once when angry heard
    I'll have to divorce you
words of searing pain not enough
to console the loss
no feeling left
    to explain the harshest Truth
she couldn't love me longer

Because of my mania, not taking pills, acting weird etc.,
close to divorce three times.

Divorce

    I must divorce you,
    you said when mania loose
    Tenth vow, *must do better*

Death

Death will not part us
Marriage vow an outright   lie
Joined now forever

Playful

When we first learn to write a language, we're taught rules and vocabulary which we use to communicate whether in speech or writing. We want people to accept, trust, and respect us. When they do, they cry, laugh, shudder and so on. That only comes if they believe us.

To be believable a poet must speak or write with authority. One must know the language rules in order to break them. This allows changes that achieve clarity, specific effects, or intended reactions. Even lies must seem factual. Think sci-fi for example.

To compose a poem with authority, poets throw out rules. He or she chooses vocabulary or makes up what they feel is necessary. Maybe makes new rules. Imagination takes over.

FUD & FUBAR walk into a bar

see no bartender
counter sign reads, "Do not cause trouble"
Glance at each other, reading minds, start to fume after
    grueling day laying mines in killing fields
Need my whisky sour! FUD shouts
FUBAR screeches, *Yeah, how's a guy get a drink?*
Voice yells, ***KEEP IT DOWN!***
so's they whisper
Told ya, jackass, it's fucked up everywhere.
and hear, ***Except here assholes.***
Didn't you see the sign over the door?
This is **The Optimists Club.**

Arrogance of Seagulls by Marion Pollack
Published in *There's No Rush*, copyright 2024

A Seagull with Vladimir Putin eyes
slightly crossed, struts by
looking for prey
Proud head bobs from side to side
eying our blanket
Steely, stealthy, diligent, he takes his time

With pointy laser beak he steps boldly
over the line
attacks the chips
Everyone curses and screams
at his arrogance and power
But he is gone
The rich march onto the beach
with the finest straws and dresses

Caviar fed kids clamor behind
kicking sand on us without concern
"Here's a good spot!"
"I don't like it!"
"Where's your good spot then?"
"Right here!"
Am I invisible?

Plop, plop go the Birkenstocks
To hold the blanket down
Plop, plop drops the cooler
Twist twist grinds the umbrella into the sand
Spray spray goes the sunscreen
polluting the purest breezes

"Alex, stand still so I can spray you!"
"No, I want Mommy to do it."
"Mommy is resting"
"I don't care, I want Mommy!"

Scream scream, stamp stamp
Sand flies in my eyes
"Little boy please be still" I say
Mother awakens like a sleeping bear
"How dare you yell at my child"

I am silent.

Wealthy grandpa lumbers over
to join the party, very tan, very wrinkled
bringing a basket of toys
"Yay, yay, grandpa is here!"
The fat, hairy belly jiggles
above his shorts

Who knows what lurks beneath.

monetized eyeballs

5-second video, stormy pics
provocative **bold** A to Z words, clips
flash on TV news channels, radios
just get a glimpse with no full taste to savor
who can afford to spend time
investigate in-depth
except long segments on NPR and Terry's
interviews or Ken Burns documentaries

attention shifted this new millennium
papers shuttered, thinner, journalists fired
home deliveries cut, digital producers choose
only online versions, advertisers reap larger profits
from slick copycat repeat repeat pop-ups ads
I close dulled eyes, stuff cotton into ears
nose still smells their stinky cheeses

what nice mounds you have...

grow tiny tooshies
in mommy's womb
that will appeal to roving eyes
   cheeks morph
first skinny then round
weight adds shape, firm curves
   youths show it off
shake, pinch, twerk it
part who we are
proud of our behind's worth
   these may be shaped
like ripe smooth honeydew
round as watermelons or merely average
   turn flat at age 50
once enticing curves vanished
so women stop swerves
by then no one scans
shrunken gluteals again
fizzle fizzle fizzle
   when young long ago
snuck sneaky doubletake butt glances
but once mister old age squashed firm muscles
ill health melted and vanquished catchy bungs
   please help, when strong enough and ambulatory
just lead me to bathrooms or lavatories
   sitting alone is what I was made for

Yes, Virginia, lead still exists

Computers are ship anchors
naughty children should avoid
unless Santa brings software

I swear

my wife is native Italian Barbie by the way
her perfect body, arms, hands, fingers, point, wave
words live and fly like watching a Rome *poliziotta*
orchestrate scads of Fiats, Alpha Romeos, walkers
    she engages strangers, store clerks, waitresses
children, babies, youth, adults—best friends for life
as if neighbors next door had extra key to our house
words, smiles, firm handshakes, laughs, winks, hugs
like Ryan Gosling driving a Mary Kay Cadillac
along Sunset Boulevard during Carnevale
    every person cherished and fine student-friend
interesting, whole, complete, worthwhile
for no one knows who they'll become, maybe
Bon Jovi, Helen Reddy, Dr. Quinn or a Roebling
NFL player, soap star, professor at Princeton
    her genes ninety-eight percent British
bubbly, permeate waking hours together,
troves of interesting facts, 5,000 iPhone pics
solid conjectures, *Jeopardy!* Daily Double guesses
    must be her once long curly red hair, freckles
unforgettable acumen that unravels universal secrets
twinkly brown eyes emit conversation starters
she recalls each person's chance encounter
    my wife surely the Italian Barbie mezzo-soprano
her romantic operatic heritage in 3,000 dialects
weaves bonds of affection with strollers past and new
praises successful friends, ex-students high and low
    when they outshine her, posts Facebook 👍
retired now with umpteen admirers
her irrepressible comradery emulated
a proud link to such a contagious personality, hear
ever-ready words of advice from her cute button face
creases around smile-filled eyes, lips, rosy cheeks
when stand beside her in ACME check-out lines or
Kohl's Cash queue at Hamilton Marketplace

won million-dollar jackpot

State took 8 percent, Feds 24 according to them
super privileged to live here in unparallel luxury
but guileless fast-talkin' shysters descend
crawl out under hidden cockroaches who cry,
Invest with us! Earn 400% more! As if

these double assailers, sly phone-tap schemers
like unknown unwanted doorknocker politicians
spell trouble for credit and bank account savings.
can't stand their blank answering machine messages
their *Get rich quick* phone calls every 10 minutes
I'm afraid to pick up, or be sucked down with lies
slicker than greased Kentucky moonshine
must change cell number, FIOS, landline
number on front door

worse case, move
Florida's The Villages huge, get lost there
drive go-cart, shell out association fees
live incognito   what?!
found me the bastards
no choice but to change name
relocate again   this time Toledo

The Language of Cancer

hand motions, pointing fingers, slaps, table pounding, grunts,
moans, choking, drooling, oversleeping, restless, hot, cold,
pleased, mad, strenuous, shaky, unstable, trippy, can't walk, talk,
swallow, Peg tube juice sustenance, liquid meds not pills or
tablets, Mayo Clinic too damn far away, too old for St. Jude's
how a positive frame of mind remains in her attitude
    beyond human comprehension, only eternal spirit
    out from under horrible black thumb knows

water runs

away, away, don't know why
    haven't chased it today
but when take a seat
hear it gurgle, squirt, pleat
surmise it doesn't like peeks
    at my pasty-white cheeks

no one's hated my butt like that
    since younger brother Stephen
when blocked the bathroom door
with him inside an hour, more
he cried, begged, shouted, screamed
    I laughed aloud on kitchen floor

maybe he told the throne gods
    what cruelty my animal nature did
maybe it's their message I hear now
Get off or be swallowed down
then where would I dump?
    outside in forested bushy clumps

only one solution, pick up the phone
    dial Fred—the fixer—neighbor's plumber
he comes, listens, confirms prison escaper
sets to work, soon hear whooshy flushes
    Voila! extra running sounds depleted

it wasn't Thomas Crapper gods at all
    or hapless, helpless, brother's revenge
just a two-bit, worn out, plastic red-coated
three-dollar Home Depot rubber flapper
    whose replacement
    can never bring him back
    from HIV AIDS permanent grave

Ellen's Underwear*

warm spray, cozy shower done, towel off
place right foot in, left, pull up elastic band
your black modal polyester clings to skin
fits like fuzzy silk, sleek, slick tights

printed label says *Ellen DeGeneres Show*
jumped out loud when you frightened guests
dished foolish pranks, played crazy games
went online, bought a Christmas pair too
Kelly green, yellow pines, red buttons glow

every morn push Winston left out of habit
countless males dress left like that, or right
the mid-thigh cut calms, molds, comforts
hairy loin, hips, joints, thighs, halfway to knees
wife's waistband letters in Sharpie graces tag
IDs you in Jersey mental clinics as mine

first bought you 20 years ago
after saw your TV store commercials
threw out dull white Jockeys, Hanes
excited to make modern torso change
you never faded, flayed, or disappointed

feel more like a man every day
wearing Ellen's underpants

* First published in *The Thursday Poet's Anthology*. This version
revised.

decisions decisions

as his only living son
   must make California arrangements
call mate often 3,000 miles back home
   from end table with black rotary phone
let her know *Okay, honey*
thrust headlong into death's derangement
   to decide next steps at 29, too young
order flowers from us and Grandmom
Funeral Director sets up viewing service
   talk to Uncle John, Aunt Charlotte
they'll tell Cousin Donny, fill him in
only three blood kin out here besides me

check his desk for bills—*Time* overdue
checkbook, just four hundred
   A will? of course not
page through little black book
Call some of his 50 floosies?
   of course, no
Sell his midnight blue Impala
 or drive home cross-country?
   one, a roaring Route 66 road trip
or else a boring 4-hour DC-10
   always the lady or the tiger

*On the passing of my bachelor father in California, age 50, of a
myocardial infarction asleep in his bed.*

Loss of love

The deeper your love
deeper the fear you'll lose it
Requited love binds

Boyhood inheritance

Miss Anonymous
    I thought
no idea who she is
perky red flared dress, long tan legs
brown stringy hair *wig?* fine young face
    Missus?
cousin Donny asked if I knew, intrigued
probably wanted to ask her out
    Shudda looked for a ring

Dad always said
    Junior, treat women well
before he croaked in bed at 50
asleep in well-worn gigolo dreams
ironic as I scream
he loved them all,
briefly

half-vow to last longer

Dad's viewing, September 1979, Santa Ana California.
This mysterious woman was the only person who came.

If not happy now…

what day are you waiting for?

    Only so many
    Pack up your kit bag troubles
    Smile girls for a while

Among the Wild by Patricia LeBon Herb

It's a wonder to catch a glimpse
of the animal wild within
that hasn't been punished out of us.

To yawn like a cat, lick a plate clean
to hear an ancient primordial scream
of a soon-to-be mother.

To receive a love-bite short of blood,
to roll down a hill with your cubs.
Morning yoga, downward-facing-dog,

a sun salutation.
Pulling socks up in the morning
taking them off at night.

You slide open the back screen door
walk out to the crickets and evergreens
give out a howl under a crescent moon.

When final rest comes
you'll lie down with the lichen, toads,
night crawlers; fastidious ants.

Smell the mushrooms in midnight grass
Aaaah. And then you'll remember,
remember—

the wild in you.

Muse for a Poem

only takes an hour to crank
a poem from fingertip mind inspirations
one large coffee to draft
one medium more, polish and craft

not enough daylight hours to type
what's inside boiling sinews
songs, ads, news from radio heads
inspires lines and books to be said

a memory, odd, or not-quite-right sight
imagination, sounds, whispers, fright
all fodder for new poetic formulas to
manifest spontaneous lights in dark nights

words, phrases on paper or screen
easy to title, convey in metaphor scenes
think and type much better in phrases
than ever spoke aloud in conversations

images, words, ideas, poems leap from more words
joyous fun to ruminate, compose, cogitate
to me each as lovely as Joyce Kilmer's tree
it's quite alright they're only just okay

His *Hallo!* cures the world's woes

The best help Joe says
 is at the end of your elbow
He states it often as we talk religion
 Italian Caruso music, Capitol politics
Used to tell irreverent jokes, diatribe poor legislators
 housed around the corner until I said
Joe, unnecessary to use the eff word
 Since then he cleans up his patter and schtick
while I sit in his raised black chair and snicker
 He calls me Reverend on barbershop visits

a foreign car

can't imagine how heartless
when they skin my Civic
such a decent automobile
more than once in a while

drivers are behind wheels
however much
they deserve a DMV lesson
if going to kill themselves

robbed at McDonald's

heard a tale on John DiBella's FM radio show,
behind cars in long line ordering hamburgers.
man behind beeps his horn incessantly
impatient, irritated, anxious to go.
woman ahead roiled and thought *What do I do*

at window woman told clerk,
I'll also pay for the mean horn striker behind.
when the obnoxious beeper went to pay,
they told him her kindness. he sheepishly
waved goodbye to mystery benefactor, scooted away

the driver behind him pulled up at window
to pick up two bags of burgers and fries.
I'm sorry we have no order for you,
the man who just left took that one too.
now tell me what was she supposed to do?

had no receipt, the other driver took it,
could only pull out, get in long line again.
did she curse and gnash her teeth?
a foolish notion they'd serve her free

or learn her lesson and slowly realize
it was McBurglar's day at the register

Americanisms

Background, smackground, we come and live from somewhere else originally, or our parents did, or theirs. Where we live has to do with how we experience culture and society and view the world. Unfortunately, it's "nation first" at almost every level.

Sane patriotism is healthy; unbridled nationalism is death.

Consciousness of one human race, not four, six or hundreds, is the realization that human existence depends on universal welfare, prosperity, and unity to overcome severe threats from man or nature.

These poems touch on the USA.

If I had your AK-47

I'd strip off the wooden stock
use it for firewood
stoke the fire in my kiln
melt down the steel
pour the blue-grey liquid
into an aluminum lamp base
let it cool, electrify it
add a white shade
give the fixture to my daughter
for her living room end table
accept her thanks then relax
flick the switch
thumb through the latest photos
of my toddler grandson's poses
then smile and imagine
your frantic search...
shocked look...
when realize it's...
g o n e

America's couple

not John & Jackie since Dallas, nor Don & Melania
music's king and queen Beyonce & Jay-Z either
nor J.Lo & Ben, Hollywood's ex-power pair
Kathie Lee & Regis split Manhattan long ago
Kelly's Michael & Ryan *LIVE* history

none top *Wheel's* continuous 40th run
since '75 it's nation's favorite TV pasttime
genius Merv conceived it and *Reached for Stars*
picked Miss White to turn his alphabet squares

Vanna wardrobe mania fast captured
fashion designers' 8,000 delights while
Pat returned from hiatus for piques at
nighttime jabs, patter jokes, and syndication

begun on prime time on NBC's peacock
V and P not just VIP's but certified U.S. icons
9 million guessers tune on E, C, M, and P Times
format copied down in twenty countries

hold my breath for witty replacements
maybe Dana Garvey & Miss Haddish get a nod
or Ken or Mayim jump *Jeopardy!* gangplanks
or shock of shocks, producers try new faces

you and I might then have a shot to earn
18 mil per annum in salary contracts and perks
but alas, Ryan the perennial go anywhere host
does a bang-up job now like *IDOLs* adore

Vanna's chore of course
still turns audience heads

Treasury Tower

we have wazoo $$$$ to fix it
162 million tax returns keep us afloat
    regardless of borrowed debt, high budgets or
what the Fed does, we fudge it.   to get
whatever we want we make shit happen

twenty-three years ago, the eleventh of Virgo
hijackers took us down 3,000 notches
    Manhattan and Pentagon families inconsolate
quick or patient, we struck back incognito
    found and shot terrorist hero Bin Laden
    now buried like the few body parts of loved ones
    we could find   problem though—
we made him a martyr too despite newly dug Arlingtons

ISIS planned years, down to the takeoff hour
    we waste time, money—campaign, spin elections, advertise
mealy-faced politicians espouse peace, security, wealth,
education, jobs, SWAT, better wages and health
    30-foot walls too, but reject bills to finish them—
only tax cut promises or tax credits win votes

if don't stop reasons for attacks troubles continue
    boil, fester, erupt, exacerbate issues
Watts riots, Occupy Wall Street, Me Too upheavals
school shootings, assassinations, crime, violent protests
    climate heat, fires, wars, terrorists, the horrible rest
35 trillion in debt, too damn Yankee proud to admit
our oppositional system rife with lamentable defects

    every hour the do-nothing partisans orate
    pontificate in front of cameras for sound bites
our proud Patriot's Day Tower totters
    verbal reminders it's closer to collapse

americans run

I'm an avid follower since 20 ought 9
my coffee run spot no longer just known
for Boston cream, jelly, chocolate frosted
colored sprinkles when added, or glazed
like my eyes behind this steering wheel in line

2019 saw tired old cop joke donut store's nickname to
plain ole Dunkin', the new pied piper of Hamelin
at the window who hands hot sipped cups to
customers from 5 a.m. well past bedtime

after downing preferred hot brown-tinted liquid
follow my light roast sweet tooth flute
straight home to porcelain urinal or john
or wherever find one on route 33 or 531

not picky when loin urges say *stop here*
if don't find release, bad for diuretics
glad yellow streams pour out straight
thank God not laced with brackish red
or have heightened concern, dread

as long as sunlight color comes from down there
don't need no snaky hospital hose catheter
will run again to five nearby drive-thru's if closed
or six blocks north to 7/Eleven and Wawa
friends give me 24/7 emergency java

Marketing 101

Big bucks buy secret
formulas for sales success
Free: OPEN YOUR MOUTH

animal restaurants

Jewish deli on Houston dishes pastrami on rye
slabs of spicy mustard, dill pickle on the side
red-haired foxes paw Mel's reserved tables
fearless rabbits chew sweet bell pepper leaves
while irate backyard gardeners watch in panic
lying in wait to shoot off small caliber rifles

squirrels order ripe round acorns, slathered
in apricot jelly or strawberry jam from Panera's
bakery bistros halls in crowded suburban malls.
crunchy peanut butter smears buttery Ritz crackers
to fill tummies of grey mice at stroke of midnight
as they crouch behind closed kitchen cabinet doors

deer jump wire fences, munch bushy violets
elderberries, browse, forbs, and mast tasty lunches
which homeowners thought they protected.
all-night Grub Shacks welcome waddling skunks
anticipating bowls of beetles and grasshoppers
to quell over-hungry nocturnal appetite shoppers

sharp-clawed snout-nosed moles tunnel
to Sixth Avenue Trattoria for insect-covered
Sicilian pizza and sips of Bull energy beverages.
sniffing animals guzzle daily city water from
24/7 flowing hoses next to every Friendly's
Chipotle, Applebee's or Mickie D's Megastore

if only these thin poor people, tall or small
street homeless could easily find
free ready-made food and drinks inside
instead of being ignored, kicked aside
trying to survive society's opulence
unlike Wi-fi app spoiled Americans
who tap credit cards, iPhones, or Androids

Night Sledding by Donald Proffit

I wanted a toboggan,
something that could hold a bunch,
a bunch
you could hold on to
speeding down the slight hill
at the old orchard in winter.

But all I had was a flying saucer,
an aluminum disk with two strap handles,
that tangled in the elastic snaps
securing my mittens;
the sad excuse for a sled—
my parents got me instead.

There was no controlling it
as you went down the slope.
It spun in spirals
cutting off sledders
in mid-course, avoiding gnarled trunks,
dented, it didn't feel
like sport at all
dinging over sledders' wakes
and hidden tree roots,
each jolt coursing
through my snowsuit
as I bounced over moguls of discomfort
in the dark.

Flexible Flyers,
something you could steer,
and toboggans in control
leaning from side to side,
all shunned their turns
each time I climbed the hill
to start again
only to crash and burn:
a meteoric disaster

in an aluminum
flying saucer.

Conundrum

Bucky in his top-down MG
drove her wind free through hills and valleys
    college bound senior, popular, gay
also had Avi's Jewish self-motivation
adoration, until summer's last dance.
  mystery though, puzzle with no solution
    she met moi propping up gym wall
lowly junior classman, not a thing to offer
no A's like she, or car, cash, salaried job
    California reject kid, low class loner.
but she, modern Alice, curiouser and curiouser
loved riddles, crosswords, challenges
    so held hands, walked out of the hop
kissed her red-headed cheek freckles
    Mmmmm, just the right touch
no human trappings intervened
    the rest home slide show history.
joined spirits, explored God's happy destiny
married, embraced, sacrificed
    forgave the past, enjoyed our present
future melded, bonded with children
  grandkids

one soul, one family entwined
type entry into Ancestry.com registry
puzzle no longer a dead-end mystery

death shucks over 50 bucks

per license to sell high-powered rifles, AK-47s
Glock pistols, shotguns, hundreds of firepower choices
destroyers/maimers/terrorizers of humans/children
school teen innocents, normal family lives broken
prosthetic arms, shot out eyes, granite gravestones
gun show cash, straw buyers, all potential killer synonyms

costs five Hamilton's to sell legal retail death
imagine Walmart's pleasure for buttstock ammo sales
car trunks open in sketchy neighborhoods
organized crime, serial numbers filed off
drive-by shootings on streets, highways goin' 65
unsafe if Asian, foreign looking, female or assaulted
black, young or Latino too, even law enforcement

banning 2nd amendment won't change behavior
or lessen constitutional rationale
Alaskan hunters, cabin owners fight
wolves, Kodiaks, 100k black bears
starved carnivores prowl backyard
ducks, geese, deer, foxes, turkeys
pheasants in the brush taste good on campfires
may be sport or self-preservation
except for Harry W's face
marred by VP's pellets

anything goes in war zones
anonymous or named dead humans' called
collateral damage euphemisms
don't warrant empathy, could be me
America at war before Bull Run began
3-9-3 million guns today, 250 million over age 18
with 2 each soon, just poll the 4 mil in NRA
youth, kids, ask, beg, steal, misuse triggers
not surprised by Columbine sacrifices
Sandy Hook won't be deadliest education

Silent light, Holy light

Silent light, Holy light
All is calm, all is bright
Round yon signal, auto and car
Holy stop bar, seen from afar
All is calm, all is bright
Round yon virgin, mother and child
Holy car seat, tender and mild
Doze in heavenly peace
Sleep in driverless peace

Silent light, Holy light
D.O.T. hold's thy might

Red or yellow splays
 from thy face
Daylight and nights
 of shining grace
Hark the Stoplight is
 born!

Hark the Stoplight is born!

Silent light, holy light
Drivers don't quake at thy sight
Zoom through red for hellish sake
Troopers hard pressed to catch the snakes
Yellow is green at thy birth
Yellow is green at thy birth

There once was a man from Hershey

who typed chocolate recipes for posterity.
What did he spy, but a fast crawler up his wall,
three inches long, two wide, scared him silly.
Grabbed a fistful of Kleenex, crunched up a ball,
shot out his arm, attacked rapidly with speed,
crushed a hundred nasty legs on the fat _____

The Most Great War

Is coming
If we let it happen
If ignore portents, clear signs
  how people feel
Oppressed, poor, sore, tired of BS
  pissed they can't be free like
The happy few, gifted, educated, wealthy
  those with enough to
  hide bad news from their ears, eyes, pocketbooks
Unlike me, you, they buy a novel
  plop in bed on comfy satin, relax, fluff pillows
Won't tear off warning label under legal penalty
  think their world today all that matters

be proud

    accomplished great firsts
    time and time again and again
    won royal freedom battle in yorktown virginia
    democracy cemented in pa state house
    flight proven in dayton ohio
    league of nations founded in san francisco
    eniac lit up in penn's moore school building
    civil rights act passed under dc capitol dome
    giant leap for mankind on sea of tranquility

    not just new laws, morals, words, movements
    inventions, better ideas, spirituality at their core
    our achievements affect living generations
    america's best, its shiniest stars
    entrepreneurs we could share with the rest
    from our little-known towns of progress
    in oregon across to jersey pine barrens
    the breath and width of this great nation
    instead push discount sales in online marketplaces

Big Red's Legacy

Singer fair, maestro of rodeo 18-wheeled bulls
Red hailed from Vegas with blue chips and Elvis-
impersonating hips

The lore begins in '57 when broke down in
Flagstaff on midnight run to Sears along flat and deserted
Texas panhandle.
  His rig sputtered, coughed, died on fresh laid asphalt

Tons of transistor radios crowded his yellow semi.
  Known for mischievous grins, long hair, Levi's blue & thick,
red/black plaid flannel shirts, under bushy rust-colored beard,
he called *Breaker, Break* on his CB

Three haulers with heavy loads on dark sleepless ribbons
headed his way, eager to help, commiserate
  Arrive, pull over, they hit it off quicker than moonshine clouds
clear blue eyes. One has skill, fixes Red's rig

The caravan buys liquor to party fierce on desert floor
Drunk on Johnny Walker they forge sandy firepit in
secluded desert gorge
  Red empties his trailer first, cartons of Sony TR-63s, his friends
toss in paper, 10 new stoves, Proctor & Gamble lotions,
razors, f l o u r, talcum powder

What the hell, tell 'em loads got hijacked, they cry. Red pours
whiskey, gas, atop the pile, lights matchsticks.
  Whoosh! Loud guffaws and slaps follow fiery *pop pop pops*
under star blanket sky, white flaky dust encases their wild
midnight prances and hi ho dances

Since that day, on July's anniversary, truckers gather from 48
states, celebrate freedom from mind-numbing long hauls.
  They chat in air-cooled rigs, swap frenzied road trips with
booze, weed, laughs and traveling women companions

Big Red's celebratory memory
A 5-day burning rig riotous raucous ruckus bonanza

I am not a cook

that's what some thought they heard
him say on oval office cameras
addressing the nation in '74
but didn't believe big news doubletalk

you may disagree, you can,
whether Watergate tarnished
R.M.'s reputation. the 18-minute
gap presented damning evidence—
an order to break into DNC H.Q.
doubt Nixon troubled by that
sharp listeners thought he misspoke
much more embarrassing by far
was his real script *I am not a cook*

Haldeman's circle of dirty tricksters
hired Deep Throat to throw press off his secret
failures in Pat's kitchen. how unmanly to
admit one can't even open a can of
Hormel Chili and heat it in a pan.
husbands like me appreciate why he said it
took the fall for what wives know
darn too well about their husbands

How you's doin'?

Says Tony to Paulie as he drives him to
  Doctor Melfi's office on Bloomfield Av
On the way they stop in the *Bada Bing!*
Though early, Tony cops feels of girls titties
  while Jennifer simmers on her well-used couch
Not good to keep female psychiatrists waiting
  they'll bore inside your cocked head

horsedrawn carriages

riders on the purple sage by dawn
yield, merge, slow, construction signs guide right
under storm-tossed clouds by night
thunderous crashes, dents, flashing red lights
four-wheeled herds moo, speed out of sight
in superhighway F-150s, gas cars and Teslas
stalled and backup lines as far as eyes see
herders skirt irate drivers' upraised fingers
weave to work undampened, press their pedal
pedestrians watch out! bicyclists' scoot!

behind mostly white, black, silver grills
inch closer to plastic rear bumpers ahead
chrome-cast logo ornaments proclaim
dealer label, symbol, trademarked brand
Bronco, Mustang, Colt, explosive Pinto
blue collar or white want to arrive in time
rush rush crush, today's Indy 5,000 mantra
tailgate, push, switch lanes to avoid troopers
pay diddly-squat to common courtesies
then sip lukewarm Mr. Coffee, yell about traffic

while wild west stallions, mares that follow
unaware of high roadway/street confusions
horse farms fenced, barb wired, posted
triple crown winners sold for semen
new cars much less once driven off the lot
repairs cost more than arm and leg prosthetics
mileage rates for leases quadruple costs
yet still, age sixteen to 101, must drive crazy
you can take the horse from the man
but not the man from the horsepower

Surreal and real

We have triggers, within us and external. At times, uncontrollable responses, impulses or thoughts move us. Spur of the moment emotions of love and caring or fists of rage. Maybe delusions.

It might be mania, and we remain unaware.

Some pieces here are based on mine. My life-altering first episode occurred in '79; a release of pent-up emotion after Dad's death. My sixth, in 2016. Thanks to wife Janet, friends, kind bosses, good doctors, and 20 pills and vitamins a day, I remain stable. Like cancer, bipolar disorder may enter remission and not be seen, but may return and flare up at anytime.

Bipolar is never cured. But it may lessen with age.

I Hear Voices

my voice
when rational
His Voice
when insane
IT's Voice
not me nor Mine
one sure source
must explain
deeper than experienced
soft yet clear
dark yet light
commands obedience
hear, act, reject consequences
but damn… so rare
when no voice at all
being/becoming cease
only IS exists

In-A-God-finda-Da-Vida

Don't kid yourself butterflies!
Every song, music, lyric about love
Sex, closeness, longing, remoteness
How we get together, fall apart, return
about man, woman, beauty or body part
Flirts, crushes, lust, any feeling we imagine

Every I wanna hold your hand
Every request to take my last name
Only shows one thing:
A soul crying for, needing, wanting true love
But it is never found in flesh or bone alone
or curved leg, sumptuous lips, handsome face

Every he, she, they, holds realities we can't grasp
Love has 10,000 names or only One:
The true object of every human heart—divine love

Songs of Earth

Oh, sweet tyranny, thou dost rule my heart,
captured my songs when first we did flirt;
now years joined, our bodies, souls shall neer part,
eulogies said, can be laid in hard dirt.
Free to roam land, air and sea arm and hand,
chat with kin, friend, ghost, stranger as if one,
no walls, borders, amidst our singing band,
His promised will for earthly life now done.
When people believe joy lieth up there,
if cherish each other's hearts like we do;
wide smiles, welcome songs, kind words will be shared,
spirits join, souls bond, lyrics one tune.
    Peace from above on Earth secure, procured,
    when believers dance, move, heaven assured

Blowing

Blowing, *chilling, rushing*
welcoming ... sensing ... fathoming
yellow suns burst into oranges reds...
enfold Us, immersive
Earth's substance dissipates ...
imbued ... permeated ... exbued ...
enter natural world
what's left dies on this hard ball of clay
mind, heart, spirit, thrills ... self expands ...
slow fashioning forms ...
inner eyes behold new script ...
one, two, three, letters ...
   Y O U
waves of hope, love, power embrace
see   feel   hear   taste
smell   touch   contentedness
   "Yes Lord"

filled with knowledge, authority over all creation —
all-merciful goodness all-loving
omniscient ...know your supreme purpose

blackness engulfs

*Reflect on my manic episode in October 1979, standing naked in
a clearing of forest, later found, arrested, and jailed.*

Waking and Dreaming

reality is chewing pepperoni pizza hut
slices with my redhead who shares
crusts and yakety-yaks while
must listen or face censure

reality is a cozy smoke in my toasty
honda 4-door at 3 a.m. drinkin'
hot wawa coffee as hum along to rock/pop
mixture on ben fm *we play what we want*

reality is eight years, six days a week, 7:30 mass
the blandness of white melting wafers on
my grammar school tongue every morning
never realizing some believe they are godflesh

reality is walking across auditorium stage
in front of hundreds of equals to receive
governor florio's award for learning to manage
myself better than staff

reality is granddaughter's hug
and *i love you grandad*
said on an eight-year-old whim
after playing dollhouse downstairs

reality is hearing *you're fired*
for disloyalty after nine years when
thought subterfuge without a thought
wouldn't get discovered or caught

reality is catching breath, holding it
as dire consequences ensure 90 dollar ticket
until red flashing lights on my tail
pull over speeder in front of my grill

reality is technicolor dream in a roomful of
gilded mirrors and my dead younger brother

waits on brocade tapestry couch with hands
folded on lap and beatific smile on his face

reality is every moment awake or
half-alert or conked out in my driveway
head on the steering wheel collapsed from
midnight until dawn sun arouses next reality

if i don't change

the shadowman chases me, running close
(i can tell he is a man)
black wide-brimmed pointy hat on seven-foot warlock
black-thick overcoat to his ankles flapping in the chase
black featherweights on his hooves
his strong bony hand held long black umbrella, closed
its silver gleaming tip points at my fleeing back
itching to stab
run harder, he behind, *thump, thump, thump...*
moving closer his black arm stretches out
that damn umbrella
ready to stab
a foot, now inches, sense searing pain
an inch, legs cannot budge faster
me, a man dressed in white, a slow quiet man
can not outrun or out scream this hell thing
a millisecond before contact, realize
he's going to kill me!

i wake, cold sweat, chastised
must do better, must change my ways
or he **will** stab me
and then…

Undying Fire

intrusive thoughts rush… fast… faster
   admonish the masses in their stopped up ears
only I can hear? the Wise Ones listen
   saints hard to find…
Zoom! Zarathustra speak! get it out, get it out
   flames inside, burn out my smarts
string of planned projects, then
   berate My toothless life…
Zoom! Mockingbird praises, highlights
   drama one minute
easy peasy on its heels, then
up, down, sideways
   fire engulfs euphoria…
ZOOM! King Solomon glances North, South
   East, West, high, low, for heaven's power
energy inside for the faith of a mountain
   the thrust of ocean 1000-foot waves…
   strength of 10,000 Hercules…
Zoom! Siddhartha's real life strikes
   walk away
sob a mile long
   down the mountain
reach the street
   sad, disappointed but true…found
I am not The Promised One foretold

In 1996, I believed I was God, king, prophet combined from out-of-control mania. Obsessed and delusional, I had split from work, told no one, secretly got my passport, got on a jet, and flew 5,000 miles to climb Mt. Carmel.

Ego Dictionary

Egoist   Care more for myself than any other human being regardless of age, skin tone, smiles, kinship, or kindnesses offered or received

Egotist Like a bad dentist cause pain in others where none should harbor cavities

Egomist   Sight and vision obscured by clouds of conceit caused by own high regard of self

Egofist   Punching you in the gut, expelling your breath, doubling you over because I am right. You are certainly wrong

Egogist   Like a geologist mines gems, polishes them so their brightness blinds, each a stone of supreme self-worth

Egobist   A baker's dozen of love I'll never hand thee, nor 13, or 9 or 3, exacting every pound of flesh to foster oblivious ways

Egotits   In love with women's flesh, and they simply must love my flesh too

Egolist   Terms of unending endearment said under others' breaths, for my superb qualities, are not ones I hear

ahh...**Egokist**
Because my love, my kiss on your lips binds thee to my will, no matter how bad I treat thee still

Egoless, where honor lies, where detachment is assimilated, prized. True humility

Meditation 1

WHAT EXISTS?
Nothing
Who exists?
Him/Her/It/
THE ONE

"The rest, is all but Leather or Prunella"—Alexander Pope's Essay on Man

Meditation 2

WHAT EXISTS?
One body/Soul/Mind
You and I
Rational Souls

"…thy eternal summer shall not fade"—Shakespeare's Sonnet 18

Meditation 3

WHAT EXISTS?
  I, said the universe
  So do I, made reply
  That fact in me
does not create an obligation

I appreciate Renatus Cartesius' Latin, "cogito, ergo sum."

Meditation 4

WHAT EXISTS?
  We
  One heart, family, clan, tribe
  Ancient, imperishable
  Like our creator's image
  Us in unity

FutureVision

thick flowing white robe, ermine-trim
clings to strong, proud square-backed shoulders
warm throbbing neck, veins in my soul
grandiose yet humble feelings flood arteries
    climb mountain steps to Mystic Shrine above
    as kings, queens, dignitaries follow behind

overhead blue shimmers, sun sky rays shine supernal
flowering gardens lush, brilliant colors eternal
multi-hued reds, white, yellow-tipped petals
fragrant cloud rose scents sweeten God's appointed mission
cool spring water pools in marble cisterns cascade clear
its flowing crystals blink in high noon's beams
look down mountain terrace
    humans recognize follies, cooperate, promote
    social justice to starving masses begging relief

faces turn upward, gratitudes profound
thanks to this New Day, peace—inevitable
joy and unity assured, hate abolished, wars ceased
billions of souls longed, pined for this surcease
interests safeguarded by just governments
grounded by sacred holy religion's spirit
home planet's two most powerful forces
civilization flourishes for next 500,000 years

    This Great Day of God . . .
        promised in His Books, Scriptures, hitherto
    Behold. Closer than your life vein!

Sitting on a terrace bench on Mt. Carmel, Haifa, Israel, 2005.
Remember major manic episode there in 1996.

Undying Fire II

Huff, huff,
climb mountain path, pause, latch onto tree
catch escaped breath
reach

undying fire
sky fills wide stare, white dome, shielded green roof
visible on horizon, clear blue surrounds soul's journey
rust-colored stones support confident feet
    His House
    Here. The Sacred Spot. Where God Passed By
stunning in grandeur, magnificent in structure
built by sacrifices of prayerful thousands
    Dare I knock uninvited?
gaze down, shut eyes, meditate, visualize greeting
ascend, scan throne of God's voice thirty feet ahead
wide white columns, closed bronze doors
nine wise elected men inside consult humbly
hear an intonation . . . low . . . deep . . . piercing
    The Tree Beyond Which There Is No Passing
time slows
stops
    No, can't pass, can't budge, can't knock
end of this manic dream
not time to begin My reign
    step aside, back, recede
no disturbances felt, no moving souls seen
no whisps of wind, no willows bend or tilt
reality strikes, surges within
    I'm not worthy
to accept the fate of Your chosen mortal man

*Note: This place, on Mt. Carmel, the Seat of the Universal House
of Justice, its nine men make a religious council.*

Daily living

Birthdays, graduations, weddings, divorces, jobs, illness, war,
laws, deaths. Everything everywhere impacts us. Piddling things,
middling things, extreme things or lackluster, we take them in.
Family, friends, coworkers, strangers. Light or serious, things
happen. We react, we act, don't, run or freeze. We experience the
life we're born into, the life we make, or the life someone else
makes for us. Every minute, we learn, grow, change, or adapt to
what or who hits us, words too. This is the world and life.

Black hat riders

Black hat horseman, silhouette under constant Sun,
shadow on every darkened night, daytime bright
Your visage stands above, heavy as two tons;
whenever light up, your menace grabs tight

Wisps reach the midmost top of my cancer skull;
streams of circle smoke rise from open lips
This Man doesn't hurt as puff slow, dull, dumb,
in curls of blue rips rips rips lungful by lungful

coast to coast millions incur doctor bills,
blank faces entombed in cast iron lung hospices
Soon off to bone-thin narrow graves, easy kills
from packs of Menthol Flavored burning licorices

Oh! What beateous air do I suck within,
cannot live without these legal horsemen
Each smoking gun sucked and stuck in
10 minutes off life's precious time

fun on a summer day by elliot m rubin

i have to find the right one
not too big
not too round
not too bumpy
one side has to be kinda flat and smooth
it's not easy anymore
my eyesight isn't what it was
then i found it
close to the shore
half buried in mud
washed it off
gripped it in my fingers
then, with a side-arm throw
the perfect stone
slid perfectly
across a pristine pond
near all the way
shore to shore
skipping
up and down on the water's top
twenty, thirty, almost forty feet
then sank to the bottom
for eternity

then i looked for another stone

Love Thomas'

English muffins so
Tasty with churned real butter
Or cheddar cheese tops

The Lawnmower

Like my Craftsman sit-down tractor with the blade engaged, or not, just blows hot air, tooling 'round the yard at 5 miles-per-hour high-speed mowing for sure, cuttin' down useless relationships, chopping grasses of once-loved memories, while raking dug up portulaca into garden labyrinths of regrettable mistakes. In my driving mad mind, the Rolling Stones push *Time It's On My Side*, a rush against the world who expects death to befall every god and creature. Round and round, back and over, sideswipe tall stalks of onion grass dreams when they should be tossed and discarded. Circle the wisteria bush vines as purple flower dancers twirl Maypoles and shop for cancer supplies tomorrow. The endless lawn seems flattened within the hour, like life born again from mommy's womb. But who knew it would take me to this suburban ranch with lily-white neighbors, at least they vote democratic. These moments in summer play over and over past ever-shorter decades, like grass grows taller and taller, never smaller, never smaller.

The Lawnmower Burning Haibun
    my Craftsman   tractor   blade engaged,
blows hot   tooling 'round the yard   high-speed
mowing for sure, cuttin' down useless relationships, chopping
    once-loved memories,   raking   portulaca into
labyrinths of   mistakes.   the Rolling
Stones   *Time It's On My Side* rush   death to
    every god   Round   and over,
sideswipe   stalks of onion grass dreams when   tossed
and discarded. Circle   wisteria   vines as purple   dancers
twirl   Maypoles and shop for cancer   tomorrow. The endless
lawn   flattened   like life born   from
mommy's womb.   who knew
    lily-white neighbors,   vote democratic.
moments   play over   past ever-shorter decades
    like grass grows taller   never smaller, never smaller.

useless labyrinths
    of Time on my Side Maypoles,
death dreams twirl cancer

Yardville Park Solitude

> FIFTY YEARS WEEDING DANDELIONS, TRIMMING
> BRANCHES, EDGING, MOWING, PLANTING CUCS,
> BEEFSTEAK TOMATOES. BELL PEPPERS

savor summer dinners, stuffed garden peppers, crispy salads, leafy
sandwiches when backyard rabbit family leaves a few pickings
 one Norway maple taller than our vinyl-clad brown rancher held a
tree fort once, but weeping willows had to fall by ax
 played grassy volleyball in their place on summer cookouts

forty lilac copses spring higher than uplifted arms to the   ,
ring perimeter, overwhelm competing outdoor smells
 stalks of white and purple Rose of Sharon guard each side
reach their bony leafy fingers into our rural blue skies
 huge circle of ivy and pines removed for labyrinth layout, now
blooms purple echinacea, portulaca, mint and pungent oregano
added to home cooked meals
 sit on patio chair as cabbage and monarch butterflies dance by

robins, sparrows, cardinals, wrens, doves, blackbirds, white-tailed
flyers visit thirty-foot black raspberry fruit tree and scarf down,
as diving jeering bluejays scare them out of their territory
 African violets big as baskets dot gardens between blue-purple
or   irises rising above our waists amid showers of low-cover
mountain pinks, orange blanket flowers, brown-eyed susans
 interspersed with four dual-spine wild white cacti columns

soft sweet breezes waft jasmine in still bushy September, the ancient
Chinese tiny flowers send its white delicious fragrance through
errant vines that dwarf, smother old-fashioned lead pole clothesline
 uniform grass height makes body rolling and sprinklers just right

six of Grandmum's stone-hemmed
gardens surround this house made from
cedar boards, more brown-eyed Susan's,
coral bells, tiny white roses shelter next to
purple gardenia amid tall rings of red lilies
       a wisteria bush big as a shed radiates
lavender-scented drips and drops into
windblown early June air where grey squirrels rush up maple tree
limbs, jump to thin springy branches in playful tail chase games high,
high, high sixty feet high and they never fall

orange rows of day lilies with long long
fronds hug rancher's side walls hemmed
by purple myrtle, purple catnip piles
cover the front views, as does 9-foot-tall
purple crepe myrtle in front
       baby solitary bees feed on pollen near
large white clematis climbing front beige
light pole. constant forest visitors bring
perpetual motion on ground alive with
possums, woodchucks, racoons, female
deer, rust-colored foxes
    Eden safe from intruders, only spirit kin here

kindly tend to our friendly guests with bread scraps, nuts, while dark
purple johnny jumpups fill empty garden spots and sidewalk crevices
as sit longer, linger, imagine paradise in every yard
    God's floral breath arrangements, we treasure nature's home

Credo of Grandpa by Michael P. Riccards, PhD

There are many fine men in Madison,
more decent and more successful,
I am just an old man who lives according
to the *tradizione,* the old way of life:
tell the truth even if it hurts;
give a man a handshake as your word;
respect women and care for children;
do one good deed a day;
take care of the poor and the maimed;
acknowledge God even when
He does bad things to you,
enjoy the little things of life;
promote friendship;
treat strangers as friends,
embrace the sun,
fear the moon,
await the change of the seasons,
and smile every morning.
Every day when I wake up I say
Grazie a Dio sono viva,
"Thank God I am alive."
There are many other codes
that will make you more money,
give you pretty girls to seduce,
provide wealth;
but life is measured by its simple triumphs,
not by its world successes.
Do well the ordinary duties of the day,
for much passes away except
a man's reputation.

Beware WYSIWYG

retail millions craftier, slyer, smarter
than you, me, him, her, any tightfisted Scrooger.
ads make it look yummy on screen and paper
but could be social media fake or scammer

you want to trust the site, believe it's okay
your eyes and mind don't lie, do they?
Yes, indeed if don't consider what
scummy humans attempt to get your money

on Amazon, other webs, flip the photos
four ways to enlarge, but can't see inside
the seller's factory, nor in what country made
when click to buy, check credit card fee

Prime maybe delivers quickest and free
tempting to subscribe for 15 bucks each 30 days
but better read the warranty and reviews by
actual users before clicking Proceed

best you can do, glean facts, tips, clues
make informed decisions not hunches
don't jump from the seat of your hot pants
you'll be pleased when it arrives intact

if works as expected, lucky to be
another contented Bezo's SOB
but if unsatisfied or not to keen
only manufacturer's defects will be accepted

remember if you want quality products
don't fall into hyped-up come-on ad fests
the best most popular dealers one and all
sell emotions, discounts, touched up graphics
be wary or be twice fooled and royally had

Where's the Maytag repairman?

drive, park, enter Wells Fargo lobby at 2 am
lobby open for anxious visitors like me
need to fill empty front jeans pocket
impatient for greenback Jacksons
stand at ATM's red stagecoach screen
big yellow letters scream
Temporarily out of order
four damn words don't need right now
Crap, next one at southern border of town
world locks portals when internet access down
until back on, hacker robbers, criminals, thieves
steal passwords, infuse malware, corrupt data drives
tracking cookies number 5,000 every hour
privacy not guaranteed for PC, iPhone, laptop
credit cards, Paypal, bank codes, mobile apps
easy pickings for nefarious cyber-attacks
better way, hook up chains to a pickup truck
drag machine away from empty money bad luck

Recycle if you care

Triangle arrows mean "Throw me in the yellow can"
   But wait!
Dig out your magnifying glass
   search for a hidden tiny number
Any 1 or 2 great for the planet
   toss me in yellow or green curbside crate
Any other digit—sorry to say
   adds tons to landfill trash mountains
Realize only 8% collected for chasing arrows
   not even close to program target goals
The CEO of P.L.A.S.T.I.C.S.
   bamboozles us again
No idea if brownfields and trash heaps can rejuvenate
   chasing arrows seems berry, berry faux to me

The man of action*

does not disclose all secrets
wise in insight when asked
he sees truth in spoken words
realizes time not ripe to share
momentous future events outright

his hearer would not comprehend
would fall dumbfounded to the dirt
reality unadulterated too difficult to swallow
not all have capacity to absorb tomorrow

ugly faults hide under apologetic smiles
crass hurts doled out rashly rarely heal
only human saints with hearts unsealed
have clear chance to express themselves

life, hard for most, easy for a few
yet all seek gold or silver spoons
soon discover wealth alone no bread giver
bodies with no souls, possess nothing to wager

every man has a secret question
Everyman has the single answer

* Inspired by: "Not everything that a man a knoweth can be disclosed,
nor can everything that he can disclose be regarded as timely, nor can
every timely utterance be considered as suited to the capacity of those
who hear it.

"Such is the consummate wisdom to be observed in thy pursuits. Be
not oblivious thereof, if thou wishest to be a man of action under all
conditions. First diagnose the disease and identify the malady, then
prescribe the remedy, for such is the perfect method of the skillful
physician."—'Abdu'l-Baha, *Selections from the Writings of 'Abdu'l-
Baha,* Baha'i writings

surf city by Joan Menapace

dripped & patted
by small hands
golden sandcastles'
lifespans depend on
seafoam green waves who give & take
on a blue planet never still

shells seaweed stones & bones
if you hold your bucket just right
in the undertow
you can capture bits of
your own ocean for your moat with
sand crabs to guard it

but they cannot hold the line against
beachwalkers
near-naked
cocobutter-coated bodies
eyes shuttered by sunglasses
shadowed by visors
can't tell a castle from a dune
lady thighs pucker
boobies bounce
the pleasure parade
sun on skin

teen girls squealing & bending
pull suits down in the back with
their index fingers
teenage boys yelling
shoulders flinch with each step
arms straight at an angle
hands spread
feet burnt in hot sand

no one gives a hoot nor a holler
about the castle & its sloppy moat
it's erect fence of scallop shells
the little ones spent the morning collecting

except for the old man in the straw hat
who sits alone in his green & white
webbed aluminum beach chair watching

Battlefield love

fights with daggers, stilettos, shives
between equal wedding day protagonists
become unsteady, unbalanced, lopsided as
fading intimacy slips through time's fingers.
blades sheathed during good moments
withdrawn when just slight digs and hurts
ready to whip out, inflict more damage in
one brief tirade or *Eff you* shouted curse

words swing out mouths off tongues like
honed swords sharpened on oil and whetstones
cut through deep protected solar plexus cores for
each knows their confidante's weak spots.
soft underbellies of misplaced hopes
hard to defend once intimacies revealed
each reads their inmost thoughts, notes missteps
skewer hearts like Persian lamb kabobs with
quick parries, lightning bolt thrusts

anger, frustration, stalemates emerge
nowhere to repair except to separate corner rooms
La-Z-Boy recliners and quiz shows nurse cuts
heal wounds before next Shiloh resumes
until, unguarded, hold hands next to each other in bed
stabs forgotten when Ken calls out answers
until grab gun from TV mantle, pull trigger
and war between North, South, resumes

Stopped counting anniversaries

Hear five words morn, noon, supper, night
Did you take your pills?
   Find new underwear on my side of the bed
      when didn't ask
   Forget to tell her opened a new business
      in only my name
   Remember my cardio appointment
      the next day. She'd never forget
   Say, *No, she doesn't live here anymore*
      to a scammer who asks only for her
   Can't stop reading her bedside bestseller on
      Kennedy's bipolar
   Scream, *No I didn't lose the Verizon bill!*
      after she accuses the third time
   Try not to let To Do List items stay uncrossed
      more than a day; or reminded that night
   Bring home Shop Rite flower bouquet, asked,
What's wrong?
   Answer the phone, hear from her room,
That's for me, each time
   Shop for Sketchers at Kohl's. She's mad;
      didn't buy second pair Half Off
Can you bring the wash down? repeated
      every Saturday morning
Don't you think you need to shave?
      when care less about facial demeanor
   Despite demanding boss, treasure minutes
      left next to this irrepressible leader
      educator, energy ball, helpmate
      executive secretary, mother, saint
      cares more for me than I ever gave
   Something wrong with this picture
      still search through FBI Missing Persons
      for her devoted husband

we all stop here

six years ago this month God's clock strikes four
sit on cedar bench, follow robin's grassy hops
stamp out butt on the pock-marked driveway
no concerns, no worries, no plans to go awry

feel odd sensation . . . *oh no oh no*
heart, damn heart! don't screw me now!
tightness, ache, pain acute, not felt before
chest heaves, suck/swallow intakes of air...

ugh! tight, tighter, twelve-foot boa constrictor!
rush inside dizzy, grab wallet, keys
drive to Emergency, right-hand clutches pecs
clammy, disoriented, faint at check-in desk

docs descend, wheel limp torso to machine
watch on screen, five-foot wire snakes higher
mesh stent inserted, locked coronary unbolted
return to the living, not time to leave eden

smile, muse, know every heartbeat borrowed
only in his hands can there be a tomorrow
but with more old age physical restrictions
they too will close with one last constriction

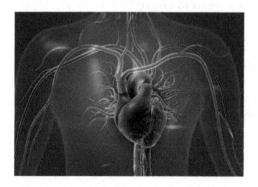

say something

our thousandth tower of silent crisis hour reached
    withheld speech, surest marriage killer besides cancer
mad, she enters CONTROL's Cone of Silence.
    used since '67 it hurts most, just because called a pal
    changed our movie date before told her new itinerary
she's doubly hurt. doubly pissed.
but as she spies dirty laundry my Friday return home trip
    her bulging black and white designer bag
    sits near kitchen basement door
Oh, you used the laundry bag I packed?
    Yeah, it worked well, reply
but placed my soiled clothing there knowing
    she'll do laundry next morning
    and I'll say *Thank you honey* to open door a crack

daily news on hiatus

    where is UPI when needed
    local headlines skip nation, world events
    only pics of garden clubs and Girl Scouts
    new fire captain installed, yoga at the library
    meaty subjects anathema with fewer pages
    no more chief editor editorials or exposés
    to chew over or send letters with views
    miss Socrates' and Aristole's weekly podcasts

don't write much

    about the rain. never wore galoshes or yellow slicker
    open umbrella only in downpours, half the time
    run through them to git where I get. its only water.
    wet for a bit, dries. do know however, without it
    pools rivers lakes seas oceans dry up, like my life

Rocking the world

In 1960s America, like other new era beginnings, a sea change happened. A youthful hippie culture and movement continued its explosive trend into the 1970s and we haven't stopped.

I graduated high school in June, one year after the summer of love. Some called 1968 *The Year that Rocked the World*, as in the book by Mark Kurlanski. It rocked mine other ways, like going steady with my future wife, smoking opium, and reporting to the Newark, NJ Army Center as part of the Vietnam draft.

The '60s and '70s were years of extremes leading into one hyperlong period. I believe we're headed to The Most Great Peace as promised. Hopefully, not after The Most Great War. This long period contains both sharp thorns and blooming roses.

Age of Aquarius

Millenniums locked in chains
recognized at last
we're millions of times more than
our country's or parents' vassals
I am young
sang Crosby, Stills, Nash, Young
nor can you kill me softly again
I am the next generation
new man, I am woman
a salve to all that's wrong
strong enough to matter
a hurricane blowing fear away
I have power, always did
freed myself from cages
of past ages
refuse to go gentle into the good night
Watch out Neanderthals!

Cream

when 17 alone in 2nd-story 2-room walkup
burned *Crossroads* into psyche's sinews
Clapton's urges shared in lyrics moved my psyche
Ginger's drum solos, guitar riffs, heavy beats
repeated on cue or off with a lifted needle.
no matter time, place, or pot-filled venues
didn't care date, plot, movie character's games
pretty faces, feeding day job geriatric patients
or pitfalls along diverted future roads
when they cried out their angst, vocals
music urged me *Find your own way*

everywhere around me a drug-induced story
emotions high, laughs drunken, uppers downed
when found divine words, freed soul at last
from society's books, all human learning
decried bone-crushing society stereotypes
slotted into each generation's molded paths.
musicians, singers, artists, sculptors
writers, poets, history teachers
created secure places in my stomach
which social order's bleeding ulcers can't breach
finally escaped Normandy Beach into *My own Zen retreat*

if I leave her alone

longer than she expects
her worried thoughts wet her bed pillows
will put *People*, novel, Soduko or iPad down
ignore *GMA*, *The View*, David Muir, Pat and Vanna
pick up her iPhone 13, text mine
where r u
only one response *leaving now*
says I will hurry

Rock It Twice

Didn't let 🎵 🎶 pass by my soul
reveled through the sixties decades twice
the first fed my long hair onto the dog
at racetrack festival outside Monopoly City
toasted live music opium, hash, beer, grass
inhaled Joplin, Joni, Cocker, Credence, Cass
landed on Luner moon 15 days later. Thirty years passed
second brought radio trivia, pranks, giveaways, trips
huffed at AM FM car stereo choices and DJs with
rapid rap curses at ads dripping *Buy me!* Casey's
Top 40 hits went the way of phone booths, typewriters.
at least fun drums, vocals, spawned Mash, Twist hips and
Macarena feet in all clubs but not my hippie wedding

Wooly Bully Wolfman Jack socked me first, his bitchin'
gravelly voice, trim beard, dark humor quips
while gunnin' Bel Air's 283 horses, prowlin' A&W
Root Beer joints on SoCal's 4-lane boulevards.
switched to staid Corolla cc engine in '79
sashayed into train station one late night July
called over red-wigged, busty Bubbles workin' the line
she sat up front, took just 25, no credit cards
tenseness released, arrived home late, greeted
8-month prego wife gave light kiss on her cheek.
guilt lingered weeks, never did repeat
told her years later after both kids split
she said *Should have expected it*

our libidos embraced musical guitar productions
Chicago horns, country turned pop/rock Miley
star-studded Taylor and her swifty army corps
hummed hot dance tunes to tap, mimic, chant
now 74 my sixties classics live strong for 6.99
a month on SiriusXM commercial free heaven

Give it Time

Topmost precious gift
of Earth's quadrillion treasures
Children second most

Lose it or save it,
don't give yours away loosely
Abuse it and die

Takes brass balls to reach
everyone with your message.
No one likes pushy

drivin' the danger highway

maybe if green lights turned red
not yellow first as they do
we'd be alert, cautious, considerate

maybe if hoods had cameras
connected to DMV data gatherers
we'd catch reckless yellow squeezers

maybe when too many points
tacked onto drivers' licenses
it turned off ignition keys, well…

maybe then, race car drivers would be in
Sing Sing where they belong
far from Sunday drivers like me

Modern History Lessons

September 4th we called you Mister
until outside of class you said *Call me Bob*
Mister Chemisty droned formulas in brown suit tie
you wore Levis, wide leather belt under beer belly
long curly hair, turtle shell glasses, cowboy boots
no others had such wild spirit or poor eyesight
diehard hippie shirts, 1968 avant-garde views

behaviors slammed me three times behind bars
a naïve lost youth, juvenile delinquent
still, you spoke to us seniors as equals
unlocked Descartes, Camus, *Last Exit to Brooklyn*
uncorked bottled-up minds like Chianti
after school past 8 as your kids snored and
we all smoked weed in your Levittown home

you shared burgundy with gouda slices
swapped your naked wife for Billy's Janice
your spouse led him into your bedroom later
four of you teaching pleasure is for pleasin'
not to be chained, blocked, forbidden
enamored of your munificence, didn't rat
to the principal or you'd be fired
our history class would be without Dylan's
Lay, Lady, Lay, John dos Passos *America* or
intrigue in Vonnegut's *Slaughterhouse*

you urged, *Go march on Washington*
proud of your bellbottomed proteges, our
hair past shoulders, long colorful dashikis
we protested Vietnam like hawkish maharishis
in June we sobbed *Sayonara*
but when you first said *Call me Bob*
invited us to your home and openness
gutted convention, let fly our narrow minds
you changed world history forever

why don't i ask

what's wrong with asking
How was your day sweetheart?
i do not do so, not nearly enough
we'd both feel better, closer, if did

i'd listen to your answer
open ears and heart, feel empathy
care what work was like, who you saw
what the kids did in school today

something seals my lips, questions never enter
my mind, buried in frozen Himalayan layers
consumed by thoughts of who won
the eagles game, what you'll fix for supper

i've always been blah, disdainful,
as if a king and you bowed to my wishes
the worst is to believe I will survive
without you close, attached to my side

we can be kindred spirits, talk spiritual things
who says life's a bitch, imperfect, lonely
it could be better by asking *How are you?*
let me erase your doubts, *I do care*

praise be to the brave

volunteer soldier or contract security guard
public law enforcement or reservist
we don't see, hear, realize how you protect us
medals belong on your breast in honest gratitude
you guard our way of life, hopefully it's right
it's war that must be defunded, not you

Eternity

began life as a human when stood next to you
under sun's strong rays in Greene Grove we made sacred
in first President's state-run park and five decades since
with *Alláh'u'abhá* engraved on bands gold-plated

we paid a nickel a head for thirty guests to ogle, chew
it felt significant though didn't possess a future clue
except believed and trusted in Him, as did you
now you lay bedridden, can't walk, eat or speak
rotting diseases consume frail thin bones, weaken feet

but keen mind, positive spirit, lights untold smiles daily
whether you depart first, or I, matters not, how, why
photo proves conjoined bodies, hearts, souls, minds
clocks, after all, mere constructs of Man's limited devise

as look back, grateful to dearest friend and cameraman
who captured our noonday bond for progeny's progeny

—June 12, 1971, photograph by Robert P. Harris

Give me thangs like James Brown

In public high school classes, best to fraternize
remove dancin' feet insecurites, go neck under
cover of darkened bleachers, cheer field athletes on.
Met my sweetheart in Art, sealed deal with a peck.
Jobs tarrin' roofs, sellin' magazines door-to-door
in/outta jail and apartments, bought VW Bus for
800 bucks, cops stopped my Jim Morrison hair
Landed a public service stock clerk gig, till ran
IBM computer refrigerator-sized blue boxes of
256k magnetic core and alabaster toggle switches
Wore white bellbottoms, puffy-sleeved shirt
sandals like our orator Kahil Gibran wore
to our hippie, marry-ourselves Baha'i wedding
Left '63 bus broken down at our concrete-walled pad
drove parents VW Bug to Beach Haven's shore, passed
Lucy the giant Elephant made out of cedar and tar
Bought used Nova, threw a rod, found hillbilly junkyard
in Sourland's Hills with Chevy engine automatic trans
sat on hood, drilled block to fit stick shift onto column
Took road trip to majestic Lake Michigan Temple
along Lake Shore Drive, water hose burst, steam clouds
hid windshield, left car aside Ohio's Turnpike
Rode under tow truck's flashin' lights to hotel reservation
attended convention of 200 friends, boarded bus to Kalamazoo
floated on crystal lake, ate fine steak and baked Alaska
Boarded second cramped airless Greyhound back
never to forget sights we shared on our delayed
honeymoon splurge, a love nest adventure

Psychedelic music

No one ever skipped
love-makin' doobie parties
Our Haight-Asbury

I'm not old

Classic I tell ya   the best euphemism that fits
like all isms, it elevates my agism to respectability
    golden or flawed, fight it off with Rod Stewart sexyism.
Once a past criminal of misogynism, narcissism, racism,
    classism, ableism, drugism, alcoholism, cynicism too

but when breathed new life in, humanism born
    added optimism, goodwillism, spiritualism
a pinch of Socratic skepticism
    with survivalism at the core and
altruism beats throw-in-the-towelism any day

in youthism drove dad's salmon white-topped
Chevy BelAir on Southern Cals highway 101
it navigated me to San Pedro Bayism's
    LA Port of Entry where switched to imported Subaru
cost thirteen-0-0 cash my stock clerk salary
    in the year Earth Dayism started

years 30 through 50 passed, like phantasmagorianisms
reached retireism near 40th annual review
    awarded office, state, national achieveisms
caroused through 60isms in a stupor, but
my t-shirt receives chuckles when says,
    I lived through the '60s twice!
in 70isms now, crappy unhealthism for sure
in my 80isms will ask the Lord His Prayer
    to avoid boring vegatableism
so please don't make me
a nursing home statism
on my hospital deathbedism
instead, give me surefire Kevorkianism
in a glass of Pepsi

strange new language brew

supposedly wrote coded COBOL lit
as junior DP Programmer desk jockey
cascade indented phrases with hyphens
for IBM mainframes bits and bytes machine language
then hexadecimal conversion into client programs.
when DOS appeared learned its slash conventions

one day a Sears sewing machine lit up
our office cubicle and we gathered agaga
shows a white stick track star running orange
circles on 4 by 4-inch green screen on top a
40-pound Portable PC with lid and handle.
asked *What's it do?* didn't make it to market

now every LOTUS filename must show
8-digit alphanumeric characters
then a dot, 8 letters or numbers, dot again
must use this strange new script or
index goes screwy, lost in the mix
frustrated, can't find what i created.
simpler times never do return

*Began as a Stock Clerk in May 1970 for the NJ Treasury Department
Computer Room, worked up to IBM Computer Operator to
Programmer and so on. DP, IP, and IT "been berry, berry good to
me," to echo Garrett Morris' words on SNL.*

Pandora will release it again

No one said she died
Love in that box too, although
troubles magnify

What futures hold

Who knows? "The" future is unknown. Your future may go far. We love to conjecture, plan, pretend the next day will be there. Not ever sure, I favorite lines/epigraphs that launch me into the past, present, or future when needed.

"To a Mouse," (1785) by Robert Burns
The best laid schemes o' mice an' men
Gang aft a-gley

Joyce Kilmer's, "Trees" from *Poetry* 2, no. 5 (August 1915): 153
I think that I shall never see
A poem lovely as a tree.

Palindrome by Leigh Mercer (deceased)
A man, a plan, a canal: Panama

From 1951's *The Day the Earth Stood Still* movie, a line spoken by Patricia Neal's character near the end to the spaceship's robot:
Gort, *Klaatu barada nikto*

Bachelor

Bachelor nights spent
bar hoppin' carefree decked out
Prowl for drunken trysts

Atoms beneath sheets
cry maphrodite where you lie
Absorbed in self sex

Stardate 2023 by Virginia Watts

Swish of red doors and I am in.
It is that easy to board the bridge
of the famous U.S.S. Enterprise.
Place beeps like crazy. A sea
of primary-colored buttons.
Giant viewscreen of ebony space.
Galaxies morphing past the ship
as white-lit arrows. The wonders of warp speed.

She is there alone spinning the captain's chair
with the toe of a tight, midcalf black boot.
Gold hoop earrings, big and proud. Trademark
updo, those look-you-in-the-eye eyes,
Lieutenant Uhura, Communications Officer,
sipping Jim Beam on ice. She hands me the bottle.
Don't let the turquoise color fool you.
Romulan ale tastes like rubber.

When I dump earthen whiskey down the hatch,
Uhura grins, arches one eyebrow more naturally
than Spock, takes a long drag of her cigarette,
launches perfect smoke rings that tap dance
across Mr. Sulu's helmsman station. *You know,*
Dr. McCoy can't really cure cancer.
This Lucky Strike is a hologram.

In the late 1960s, little girls like me admired
the Lieutenant, the only female officer on the bridge.
She inspired a future of female astronauts. Our hero
is willing to get drunk with me. I can't believe it!
I stuff my body into one of her skimpy, red bell dresses.
Nice velvet, though. We take turns bending over,
mooning each other.
Hysterical. High-school-pranking-it.

She gets drunker than me. Tells me when Kirk
gets snippy and barks things like *Uhuro, are you sure*

you're hailing the right Starfleet Command? she places
a call to her cousin Subbo at his 24-hour taco shop
in Detroit. When Subbo answers *Tell Jimbo to fuck off*
she has to swallow her laughter like a cherry gumdrop.

Always overly alarmed by enemies, I gasp when a Klingon
vessel materializes on-screen. The Lieutenant shrugs it off.
Adjusting the little silver thing in her ear, she takes a swig,
hails our visitor. *Gowron, you little asshole, you better
be here to pay up for the girl scout cookies.*

in the year 2025

the second i say …dot, dot, dot
unforeseen forces impinge
futures take shape or unravel, unhinge

life alters, dreams sail by… dot, dot, dot
missions succeed, falter, fail, die
unbeknownst to hopes of woman or man

night owls hoot warnings… dot, dot, dot
unforeseeable events shriek alarm words
in black ink headlines by the scores

…dot, dot, dot react, pounce, debate, reset
should heed prescient calls to alter course
given to hungry searching creatures like us

…dot, dot, dot
the second every moment arrives
so much damn excitement!
too dull to let it pass mistaken for tomorrow

Recipe for Shangri La

World Peace
not one hope nor one glimmer
in populace, leaders, legislators, dreamers
until unity of thought prevails and all agree
history then earns its civilization pedigree

institute universal wage laws
truth in lending, advertising, campaigning
remove fear from news reports, media
domestics and foreigners share resources
scientists and think tanks, sociology, technology
not just Band-Aid Peace Corps volunteers

universal suffrage instituted, obeyed
girls, women, gay rights no longer delayed
education mandatory for citizens
equal parts academics and trades
discrimination, race superiorities outlawed
current laws primed for reform

ingredients for modernity
1 Tbsp moderation
1 Tbsp truthfulness
1 tsp consensus
1 lb democracy without opposing factions

mix in 1 cup cooperation
stir sacrifice, deprivation, sharing
set temperature at majority rule
protect rights of minorities
execute unity of will, thought, action
Voila!
Peace at last, tastes divine

idyllic obtainable

hundreds of thousands
suburban developments, manicured lawns,
narrow street neighborhoods, rundown bordellos
  ten thousand cities poised to turn 'round
    safe to talk, walk, trot, bike, push strollers
      kids, parents, grands, strangers love and say *Hallo*

billions of lanes and highways allow
crisscrossing nations in wonder
billions more jobs, daily sacrifices, free schools
food stores, deliveries, global sanitation
clean water, air, parks and greenery
no plastic trash, no spewing smokestacks
  what's so difficult about making this place
    a Disney dream park?

binding treaties, fair decisions
not arguments nor ultimatums
just laws, equal conditions
bright minds to harness solutions
  make eight billion people happy not sad
    not difficult to attain
      if bind collective minds in agreement

next New Year's Eve resolution
work together, gain personal wealth;
open hearts, minds, bank accounts
resolve issues now or die unbuilt
  nothing too difficult
    if prosperity our birthright
      expand civilization, banish doubt or
pay lip service and shout
it's mine and you can't have it!

Portrait of a Flophouse by Robert M. Berry

I had an Omen first time I drove by
Then woke with icy breath
after my first cold night
end of hall   third floor   room 2
of the Stockertown Hotel-Saloon

"How did I get Here?" whined a distant radio
cold radiators clanked and hissed
along with the Grover Twins
30 something-beer bellied-24 hour-a-day-TV drunks
while across the hall Corvette Kenny
got caught huffing spray paint from a garbage bag
'cause his Vette was repossessed
his girlfriend grabbed the cash and left
leaving him broke   wasted
a sad but true imposter

then I found Old Bill
stone cold as the radiators
dead in his bed
drank himself to death
which was sad but expected
his door and eyes wide open
I shut them both
traced a cross in the air
with reverence

I calmly notified Richie the new landlord
a mogul in the making in his get rich quick mind
who had just moved his wife and new born daughter
into the "Luxury Suite' on floor Two
above this bar cum makeshift strip-joint
where at least the girls pulled in some cash each day but
    Sunday
till Richie's wife nixed that on Monday
which justified a Goodbye Celebration
for Miss Trixie, Black Betty and Kitten

dull green chipped plaster walls oozed sad endings
in our Cloud House of incomplete souls
one bright starry night while peering
out my North facing, stuck-shut cracked window
I remembered that Omen in my bones
I breathed free and the Moon was glorious

Mary had a Little Lamb parody

His fleece white as mountain snow,
Everywhere that Mary went,
The damn lamb was sure to follow

He stalked her to Scotland one day,
Which was highly against the rule,
It made children there giggle and play
To see a lamb at a research school

So, the researcher turned them away,
But still, she and lamb lingered near,
Waiting patiently in their bay,
Till assistant in lab coat did appear

"Why does the lamb love Mary so?"
Curious jealous children cried.
"Why, Mary loves the lamb, you know."
The sly gene scientists replied

Not the first lamb to be cloned,
But the children didn't know.
Mary Einstein wanted secret kept
Since she was a clone-child too

The Alien Spoke English
Adapted from the movie *The Day the Earth Stood Still* (1951)

walkers stroll pebbled garden paths
blankets dot blue-green fields of grass
Lennon's imagine not yet installed
swoosh… the glowing grey orb descends
capital city children and blanket lovers scatter

grey-suited man disembarks, addresses gapers
his giant robot stands silent and he speaks English
I come in peace with a message
…shots ring out, one hits his arm
news travels wide on black & white TVs, radios

the alien enigma rushed to hospital
armed soldiers encircle his grey ship
with machine-gun Jeeps, armored vehicles
he heals, escapes his bed, meets a boy
young Billy takes him to a smart neighbor

the PhD knows the man proves true
suggests *a demonstration is required*
for mankind to hear you. man replies
tomorrow when hands strike twelve
at appointed time, all electricity died

no power, world shocked dumb, only
airplanes glide silent around the globe
the scientist gathers friends to listen
the man's words poised for attentive leaders
soldiers and tanks threaten annihilation

on his spaceship ramp to leave he speaks
our confederation of planets abolished aggression
embrace peace or become a burned out cinder
our robot guardians will watch, listen
he and robot turn, board saucer, speed away

those gathered stare open-mouthed
the world heard his threat
if they believe it's true
will heed his warning
or will never see the sequel

the reset blues

you appeared on my black screen of death
we've got updates for you
hope they'll protect me in this online world
we want everything to be ready, don't turn off your pc
know enough by now not to touch the keys

didn't worry until at 91% it froze
20-minutes since last budging
in front of impatient eyes, itchy fingers
if hadn't seen the rise from 80 to 91
would have rebooted out of boredom

you devour gigabytes on my C drive, your vault
you have your reasons, but don't share secret codes
why not let me custom install?
i can you know, talented enough since '92
but you don't trust my technical acumen

all the while wait, wait, wait
hell, over an hour already
then magic, home screen turns blue
color photo of grandkids at the beach
login and begin to load, reinstall, load again
15 programs you deleted wait to be reactivated
hope you eradicated the virus

ing my thing

to do is to did or done is to doing
to walk is to walked is to walking
to talk is to talked is to talking
to screw is to screwed is screwing
why then   why
is **to do** active and **doing** passive

is not to do the same as doing?
is not to be the same as being?
to walk, to talk, to screw
all the same to me whether you care
as to be and being together
each moment precious
fortuitous, planned or random

my life as i look ahead
back to the bare bones of it
any truths or tales i shared public
why do you feel compelled
to correct my tense or gerund
unless happen to be an English prick from
university who interdicts poets writing

A formidable model Rev-9

sent back in time to kill Sarah, John
—like Arnold of black leather jacket fame tried
When he left, software programmers determine fate
—mankind's survival or death beyond 2025
Maybe Grace saves us, maybe she can't
—depends how Hollywood plots blockbuster script
Either killing machines more effective than men
—or back to Stone Age without computers/internets

On Children

Our origin is the same: egg, sperm, gestation, whether a birth mother or a surrogate. Our childhoods may be similar or vastly different, but all spent learning, and growing. An innate hunger for discovery, always curious.

Any place or world we find ourselves in becomes what we made it or let someone else make. Without children there is no human race.

And a woman who held a babe against her bosom said,
Speak to us of Children.
And he said:
Your children are not your children.
They are the sons and daughters of Life's longing for itself.
They come through you but not from you,
And though they are with you, yet they belong not to you.

—Kahil Gibran

"…we must believe the things we tell the children…"
    —Woodrow Wilson

"Children are the living messages we send to a time we will not see."—John F. Kennedy

"I have a dream that my four little children will one day live in a nation where they will not be judged by the color of their skin, but by the content of their character."—Martin Luther King, Jr.

"Children's children are a crown to the aged, and parents are the pride of their children."—Proverbs 17:6

"As the twig is bent, the tree's inclined."—Alexander Pope

A Child Sings

we load the SUV as Grandmum asks
Sienna Rose in her high backseat
What songs would you like?
  Oh Raffi of course, insert CD

hear happy tunes as we head to beach
Wheels on the Bus go round and round
tires spin turning highway asphalt brown
until *swish beep* and *shush shush* when
Wah, Wah, Wah echoes cries from babies

she uses her five-year-old voice to help
Baby Beluga swim deep blue seas
after bananas go crazy with vowel sounds
baneenees and banighnighs, not to be outdone
by banonos and banewnews in staccato rumbas

Raffi rings, rings, rings banana phone
Chuckle chuckle chuckle
Sienna answers *Boo-ba-doo-ba-doop*
knows every lyric's dip, dop, beat
every A Tempo with Canadian Accent

the children sing, sing-along this day
children of the world cry tunes in play
millions laugh, guffaw, giggle and rhyme
sing hearts out and cares away
with Grandmum, Raffi, Sienna and me

Drunken Nursery Rhyme parody

Hickory Dickory the clock
Had a mouse run up his dreadlocks
A murder of crows rang the bell
Down ran black gooey gel gop

Till time had all but stopped

Fore and aft went ten Dijon flies
In a ship constructed of mustard pie
The sails flew out, ten bosons died
Planks of blue-black elderberries cried
    Till time had all but stopped

Three rowdy, blind and randy mice
Did fit and fiddle in Cha-Cha wriggles
The third said *This is terribly nice!*
Sipping and slurping liquor store Ripple
    Till time had all but stopped

Hey there middle graders, a riddle
Fritz the meower speaks in punny squiggles
Why ever did your mommy piddle
When bare backsides reddened your giggles?
    While time will never stop, not completely

Progeny

I don't know everything, but can tell alL
A daughter, son, will remember yOu
Much of what I think came from moVies
A part of 20th century personalitiEs
Motivation and inspiration thereoF
A chance to create new life toO
Nobler now since we number fouR
Of mother, dadder, and full-grown cherUbs,
For betterment of society, our love birthed **BOTH**

Kids are brutal

To love unless true
From the get-go when first meet
Love sunflower seeds

Granddad poem by Sienna Rose Richards

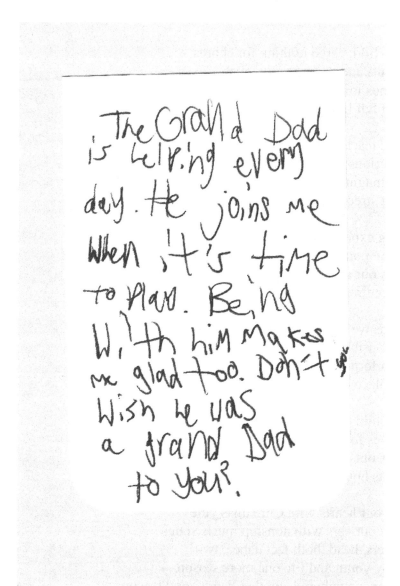

The Grand Dad
is helping every
day. He joins me
when it's time
to play. Being
with him makes
me glad too. Don't you
wish he was
a grand Dad
to you?

age 7-8

be a child again

dilemnas   choices   demands
trivial, minor, momentous
command our attention, force decisions
easy, hard, flip, flap, immediate crap

as a child, cared nothing for chores
parents and siblings took over
curious impulses guided my acts
what felt like doing dictated adventures

good teachers the keys, open our minds
as curious questions leap free
fill imagined story venues with awe
twist streetwise facts, blast away doubts

bring experiences home to mom
where ponder misplaced wonderment
open our mouths, crinkle our eyes
concentrate on freedom to roam

but as we grow tall, duties do also
responsibilities pile high as sink dishes
soon forget childhood laughter
misplace old hopes in chained up cannisters

the child within waits to escape
wishes for a happy family and pushes
pulls out paper, ink, pens, brushes
paints houses with mom & dad in landscapes

fills our hearts with Christmas yule
jams our ears with nonstop music songs
fingers, head, both feet dance, twirl
enjoy youth and life one more season
joy unencumbered, another damn good reason

Little Miss Red

She had a cute little devil
His skin redder than blood
And everywhere she went
Her devil spread poisoned mud

He went with her to school one day
Contrary to the principal's rule
Satan's spit made children laugh, play
Act silly, gay, like any hellish fool

So, the teacher tossed him on his ear
But Miss Red snuck him close and near
To poke and joke and loudly shout
Till teacher did appear in a pout

"Why does this devil love her so?"
The laughing children begged to know
"She loves this sprite to death you see"
The teacher told them facetiously

Mutual love, meant to keep together
Grabs on, won't let souls fly off kilter
Miss Red and little devil a metaphor
Life here on Earth extracurricular

Who says so?

Likes, dislikes, labels in/out/ugh/ouch/admired
Newer words for dictionaries other than awesome
Arcane stunts break records in Guiness volumes
Born during Beat Generation's baby boomers
didn't know I'd like Len Cohen's gambits
Gen X, millennials, Gen Z, Alpha dog or cat
Now we all fear their next labelled moniker
Please sirs, keep Omega at the end as our big hurrah

Boo! Did I Scare You?

when son and daughter were young
did not want Halloween night
scary costumes, thinking they might
get more candy if friendly like Casper.
No stores had signs named Costume Scene,
Party City, or Spirit Express, oh no.
Walmart's weren't anywhere near, nor Kohl's
so wife sewed costumes from fabric leftovers

our boy a bug-eyed Kermit, girl, Raggedy Ann
or he a cardboard computer, she a pink ballerina.
as a teen his Flash seemed real, or Green Lantern and ring
she too social to play children's games anymore.
now can purchase Terminator or black-robed Darth
Robin, Batman, Batgirl, Barbie or Power Ranger
Barack Obama, SpongeBob, or Freddy Krueger
Twerkin' Teddy or Wonder Woman, anyone you like

Teens today wear saggy jeans and t-shirts, carry
pillowcases for their swag. Fewer treaters reach
fewer houses, mostly driven, picked up later.
Not 1950 when every home front door light lit bright
Enjoy this Halloween as best you can
If brave, open up to our laziest 21st century creatures

Little Miss Muffet

Sat on a tuffet, reading Baldacci's latest thriller
Grisham, Atwood, Morrison, every classic
Her A to Z log page lines full of authors' killers
Kept a list since high school, a collector's collector
As teacher she read aloud 7 Harry adventures and
tons of novels, nonfiction, texts and odysseys
however not one hot romance big seller or paperback
retains her under covers imagination just for me

proud to be a dad

when born he named me J R
added S R at end of his
with mom going along
enamored, starstruck
in appearance happy

handsome, well dressed
Dad wore starched ironed shirts
called Sharpie by friends, like the pen.
gave mom weak excuses when he ditched
to cruise bars, joints, NCO clubs
eager for women and alcohol

when mom found his lover's letters
hidden beneath skivvies in his drawer
heartbroken, she remained obligated
no place for a single woman with kids in
'50s Princeton political correctness

he split anyway with a hair-dyed blonde
down two-lane U.S.1 to sunny FLA
neither saw nor heard from him again
till he and second wife Marilyn took me in
a confirmed juvey jail delinquent.
kind of him, showed something of a heart

while I stayed clean, they both split too
freedom, Smirnoff's, sex drive won out.
proud to be ex-Marine from Quantico
ex the operative word, we dated together
when died in '79, I paid for services
he was proud of me then too, I know

Relationship anyone?

To me and as Baha'i writings describe, relationships fall into four
categories. All have love as their foundation:
God to God
God to humans
Humans to God
Humans to humans. We prize and devote ourselves to this
more than any other.

Earthly heaven

Oh, sweet tyranny, thou dost rule my heart,
captured my soul when first you spoke to me;
five decades together we will never part
as God in his wisdom doth set us free.
Then shall we roam His heaven hand in hand,
chat with kin and stranger alike as one,
no secrets in our closeknit merry band,
his tasks for us on earth finally done.
Barred skeptics must realize what lies ahead
if but will love each other like we did;
wide smiles and welcoming words will be said,
"Souls melt here, minds open, wide eyes relive."
  Believe heaven on ev'ry earth assured
  when love for love's sake forever procured.

Wedding Day Leviticus

1. *Do not lie.* It upsets them, violates trust, will never be believed.

2. *Accede every wish, desire, need and want.* It may require change. It makes them happy, pleased, amenable to kisses.

3. *Respond Uh huh, Okay, I will.* Act like you care.

4. *Let them know where you physically are at all times.*

6. *Enjoy their company.* Watch Jeopardy! or Family Feud together in bed. Hold hands. Cuddle.

7. *Dress the way they tell you.* Button the lowest button on your Polo shirt before they do it for you because your chest hairs show.

8. *Compliment their clothes and looks.* "You look nice," goes beyond sexual intercourse.

9. *Never hint that they look heavy or fat.*

10. *Do not hit them with bare, raw, unvarnished truth.* It's too brutal. Women are sensitive; men are pirates.

11. *When they ask a question, be kind.* "A kindly tongue is the lodestone of the heart." — Baha'u'llah, *Gleanings for the Writings of Baha'u'llah*, CXXXII

12. *Follow up saying "I love you" with cut flowers.*

13. *Teach these to your son.*

Give

Give		your boss a hand
Under		pressure, do not freak.
Someday		you'll be them

You Are All I Need by Roberta Batorsky

Not knowing where love stops
or begins
I bury myself in you
for my hungering heart knows only
a hangdog winter.

I rush to you
with surfeit or loss
my emotions loosened
in your warming breast.

Neither art nor device
can lift this dread off me
You are all I need
to signal my new season
and nudge this frozen shell
back to life.

With you I am the hidden spring
or the shaded stalk
hesitantly blooming
where new growth stirs, shudders
and sprouts.

Sorrow yields to opportunity
to announce the looming spring
my love extends its righteous span
sighs, grows to overflow.

No Sense Arguing

I'm awake if you want to take your shower.
she states. think I took one yesterday
but sure don't keep track or check it off
while she knows I didn't without doubt
She keeps count of dirty silverware

Eat your salad, it's good for you.
Who am I to dispute her nutrition?
at least they're spinach leaves I like
cucs, tomatoes, carrots, diced onion too
After all, she's the chef each night

Fix your collar, and she
adjusts my shirt in my belt
before we leave for pizza in jeans
Who cares? I think
but she knows someone will

Change your underpants every day,
she tells me every morning
when two days maybe three is sufficient
But she does the wash, notes the numbers
therefore, comply to please June Cleaver

Female mates care for male mates
more than for themselves it seems
Sometimes wish she'd let me slide, but then
I'd never be clean, eat, look great, live long
Easier to go with the program than astray
be her loving man and obey
Gift her new pearls on her birthday

to cheat or not

every time I glance or gawk
comely women walk through my mind
who will it be tonite
maybe Renata, black-haired beauty
just joining writing class
who mesmerized me yesterday
possibly doesn't know I'm married
see no gold band on her finger either

or Connie B., six-foot blonde looker
lives ten houses down, walks her small dog
crushed hard on her bod forty years before
when both worked for a demanding employer
so easy to imagine Mister Lust saying now
Yes, do it, like Nike with the words on both our lips

would be in secret of course
can't bring her home to this shared bed
no, too full of risk
my mate sniffs out scents better than Lassie
there's the rub, where to go? have to be her place
Sleepy Hollow or another cheap motel
cash not credit card leaves no trace

God, you make gorgeous creatures
I won't cogitate on getting caught
a one-night stand always best, if could
just contain it in my pants
wash hands and let it rest

best advice, don't swoon into binding trysts
unless wish to lose the good you've got
dinners cooked, clothes washed, shirts ironed, kisses
crush these sex crazed dreams, it's for the best
wouldn't want the kids without their dad
like I was

Moon Face Senryu

Look up from my bench
smoking menthol cigarette
Moon's lungs dry slivers

Earth's shadow deep black
crooked smile crosses her face
Day returns same place

Blessed to have a chance
to put best world together
Unless piss on it

Opportunities
rife to save hurting people
Shout *Give us justice*
Get off your asses
Help your brothers and sisters
They ignore message

Sex the only goal
most human playmates live for
While moons burn fire

Sex filled thoughts will fade
you'll want a companion then
Fire turns inward

My bench now sits two
more comfortable with you
Stay here beside me

We have each other
it's now time life stayed peaceful
The moon is cool, free

The Other by Craig Sherman

A faint rainbow appears in the sky,
My ephemeral body filled with life,
My eternal soul, it cannot deny.

I capture the picture of perfection.
The voice in my head takes exception.
I've forgotten that I am already whole,
A fact lay hidden, deep down in my soul.

I strive to elicit empathy for myself;
The same as I do for the other.
There I go again up on the shelf,
Taking a back seat to my brother.

But when the other feels broken,
When their burden is weighing,
I can share a soft smile,
can hear what they're saying.

I say it's alright, I understand,
When the other has hurt my feelings.
I stand alone on the edge of the strand
Searching for purpose in life and meaning.

When scorned by the loss of a lover
I can comfort the heart of the other.
I assure them their fish they will find.
Just look in your heart—not in your mind.

When the other looks in the mirror,
I stand behind them and see the light.
Still, the beauty fades when I come nearer;
Tormented by the reflection in sight.

And when death comes to visit,
I can hold the other's pain.
Solace and comfort, I can elicit,

But for me, the search is in vein.

But perhaps in the bright morning sun
There is a truth that dark clouds can't hide.
A transformation --- once done
Will bring tears and a sigh,

The message is ubiquitous, hidden in plain sight
I hear the words in the quiet and still of the night;
Jackson sings me to sleep and helps me to see,
It's my kind words that find their way back to me.

The sand is falling fast and the mound grows high,
Not the past, not tomorrow, but now is the time.
That we can turn into our hearts to finally discover.
After all it is we, who have always been the other.

Ghost lover's voice

Love warbles love's wishes myriad ways
songs, ballads, poems, elegies and eulogies
nightingales sing in the Gardens of Night and Day
Constant cacophonies do not take for granted

pleasing to the ear's tympanic membrane
they flow through the ossicular chain unleashed
when reach its destined mate in the labyrinth

All the while Love balances head, heart, body, soul
straight to the snail-shell-like cochlea of the eighth
cranial nerve and… miracle of miracles!
I hear you say, *I love you always and all ways*

Love melts, flows into the gut, up the throat
to the tongue and hear hammer, anvil, stirrup
repeat Molly's last farewell, *Ditto*

better to say...

I don't care
instead of the eff word
it sets off
immediate shock
shuts their mouths
turns them away
shows your fed up, not fired up or angry

they stop talking when say it, or
if they're showing iPhone pics
of people I don't know
they are taken aback
don't have a response
their golden silence
what I wanted all along

only one problem
if say it to the spouse
a week of cold shoulders
goes by slow with
colder single showers
no shared warm covers or cuddles

must speak truth judiciously
save it for store counter clerks
then walk out the door

here... take it

take it all... its yours
I give it to you... freely
Everything you see, hear, can touch,
live, experience...
Choose wisely... or feel my wrath

heart sighs a breath by William Waldorf

a lump presses inside against my throat
unable to touch your love anymore
stuns my mind and to breathe feels like a chore
as lungs struggle to end this garrote's choke

numb senses bring along their lost control
first with tingles at the base of my spine
which will steal night's desire to unwind
but be lost in depression's deep hellhole,

to hear loud echoes inside a scared mind
death forces grief   trust broken like a thief
my rejection lingers without relief
to feel violated as if I'm blind.

unable to rebound from this dark depth
of existence my heart sighs a breath
tries to comprehend this to
as if
while my body aches to be held, be touched,
as sad overwhelms my desire to live
then anger saves me from execution
never surrender to degradation

neck's back of a
some
but anger as if relief
trust takes self-worth to push me off a cliff
to free fall violated

what's pinochle among friends

queen of spades and jack of diamonds
add just four points to our terrible meld
need to make, surpass, our 15-point bid
or end up in the hole, lose points times 2
subtracted from our score, insurmountable

tricks are the heart of the game
strategy, timing, luck, pneumonic memory.
these battles me and Bobby McGee need
to keep us on top, save meld and bid to win
as we sit across from our age-old nemeses
Big Bob and Spudley, characters from the hood

we've played this sport since '84 when Big
Bob and Spudley taught us. still, my discards get
confused. they exult, high five when trounce us
all in hearty jest, sure, best friends since kids
they've played us newbies as suckers since Game One

their raucous stories try to distract, but we
concentrate on each lead, solidify tricks fast.
I gather ours, Big Bob's long reach, theirs and
he either moans or Spudley shouts, his palm
slams down, *Smack,* takes our Ace with trump
those two read each other's minds, we casual
play for fun, maybe why we win. who cares

aces beat tens, tens over kings. queens,
jacks, nines, worthless. always lead highest they say
get counters from my partner, skim a king out of
Big Bob's huge paw. proceed to trump most tricks they try,
that's how it's done

taking last trick with trump can make the
difference, win, or shoot and be embarrassed
but we don't care win or lose, as revel in
camaraderie, stories, jokes, Heineken O.O.

near beer, chips, jalapeno dips, Pepsi fun

we pro wannabes reach 100 first,
not unexpected in our string of wins
the 2nd set confers permanent bragging rights
they're dying to beat us, haven't in years
means time will not run out
before next month's dining table skirmish
but who's keeping score except Spudley's
pencil and eraser and Big Bob's tears   of course

Another day better than good

Open her door, she's alert, open-eyed
Yesterday like Sir Paul sang, better past and over
Troubles can't hurt her anymore
Blood platelets confirmed raging malignancy

Each day a new challenge
Her tenacity overcomes fears inside
Riddled with cancer, survivors survive
Private and locked, no one wishes for pity

Made it this far, 14 infusion years, 2 chemo
Still smiles wide, animated, alive
Kids and grandkids adore her hugs
She turns gaga with them on Facetime

Can't speak, swallow, drink or walk
Sleepy coughs, dreams speech will return
If not, I'm happy for us honey
You woke up one more tomorrow

On Writing

A 2010 book I admire is Stephen King's *On Writing: A Memoir of the Craft.* I liked his memoir style and lessons so much, I reviewed and quoted 4,000 words from it into 14-pages with my insights added. In 2013 I sent it off to Simon & Schuster for permission to make copies for my Hamilton Library creative writers, which they charged me $6 per copy for.

In that book, Stephen wrote five sentences of excellent advice to writers about writers, and how writing wasn't about making money or being famous or other perks. It was about enriching readers and the writer. It reminded me of sage advice from the 1880s that said, "Wake up, get up, do something," which he reiterated.

I'm happy for many things. Waking up comes first. Being able to write, even if only one person, is high on my happy list. Two other excellent books on are writing well are *The Memoir Project* by Marion Roach Smith, and *Bird by Bird* by Anne Lamont. There are more now too.

One of my favorite quotes on writing is from Elmore Leonard, whose westerns, crime novels and thrillers sold millions of copies. Thirty movies were produced based on them. His realistic, action-oriented, nitty-gritty style was riveting.

That advice was "try to leave out the parts readers skip."

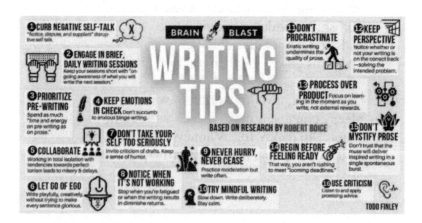

on my gravestone

chisel these words two inches high
Too much to write, you do it for me
words constant endless possibilities in
seven thousand plus languages.
lingua superbia for 21st century eyeballs

English alone has a million words
so sit tall at keyboard and screen and
self-publish a memoir since Amazon free
experiences, sights, events, you, he or she
emotions written on pages ripe for sharing

print a book every month left to live
until fingers stiff and frozen.
enough food, wine, drink and sex
to titillate, horrify, swoon, voice opinions
transcribe a hundred volumes into ebooks

billions clamor for lyrics and movies
ready-made buck 99 eBook thrillers or
rosy poems on Instagram abound
tv and book series like girls with
dragon tattoos carved in their backs.
wish there were more like 'em

don't overlook the things still free
before money-grabbing millionaires
put sale tags on everything that moves
we'll no longer afford ProWritingAid or Grammarly
be slaves to AI software tycoons and retailers

write it now   get out paper   pen
laptop or ipad, google docs or apple pages
don't let precious story time slip by
readers will learn from you, laugh
smile or cry, say, *I should write it down*

every poet writes a love poem

wouldn't be a poet if didn't.
we cherish Shakespeare's sonnets
Browning, Byron, Shelley, Naruda too
natural things to write about, emulate
forever swoon over girls' long tresses
even unrequited, express confessions
empathize and hold sobbing cries or caresses

whether or not a poet's imagination magic or
appears to just skim surface, expose
beneath the black ink on a billion pages
myriad love poem versions describing hot kisses
behind velvet curtains that transpire
when hop under sweaty sheets

join now, prepared, arranged, for you alone
let's tingle, mingle your skin, senses with mine
we'll build up slow, soft, tender
true love—never rushes to climax
it fondles, cuddles, fingers, dwells
leaves long lingering fragrances
until *Push!* can't control heated desires

once spent
you'll always taste
that morsel of true love's kisses
poets aim to share

imagination, thought, memory
comprehension, the common faculty
each step plucks love's heartstrings
while yet we breathe on the lyre of touch
that feeling a good poet's love song

dozens a day

titles, concepts, piquant observations
flow through brain's synapses, maybe NaNoWriMo
NPR topics, IMDb movie or BMI lyric snatches
what Dunkin' clerks say out orange kiosk holes
or wife scribbles on today's shopping list,
generate emotions needing max expression

jot word wisps in journals, endless pens handy
type more into MS-Word templates
blank white never phases or causes pause
lay down two, three, four verses on each page
polish lines as inner fancy strikes knowledge banks
autosave those by calendar months or age

since retired time holds still or rushes past
nice, quiet, private alone in Civic or at PC keyboard
meditate, ruminate, debate world's turmoil
don't wonder who might read, toss if trivial
if cool, post hashtags on Instagram to millions

express what's observed or heard one goal
voice saner ditties except April Fool's Day
humans that walk this planet fight over graves
too bad dysfunctional system, divided USA
it is National Poetry Month after all
sign up now. write your Poem-a-Day

Three

Three poems per minute
turn inside head, hope for gems
One memorable

Write Anything

Give me a letter like x
in exposition or xylograph Xerox
I'll bore your mind with narrative
  Give me a word like phone
We'll talk shop, kids, old times
or cry on each other's party line
  Give me a phrase like
the small bar was entered
I'll write a passive voice joke
  Give me a cliché like
time flies. I'll tell
you writers don't waste it
  Give me a line of prose
I'll show you how to use
vivid nouns and verbs
  Give me a poem's line
I'll tell you what it shows
to fire my soul
  Give me a reader
I'll write an engaging story
poem, blog, tale or limerick
  Give me a memoir
I'll demonstrate how to
publish life to the world
  Give me a camera
I'll blow your mind

Kill

Kill all your darlings
Stephen, not Tabitha though
Who will you hold to?

Selfish love

Hello, Pilot, hello Bic, hello Sharpie
 each one a rabbit hat trick
 in Basho's poem bag.
Once just blue or black,
 surprise, new colors now range
 yellow, blue, red, orange like
Highlights in my hair
 when four years old and toe-headed.
I rely on your company
 cannot compose without you.
Dare not put you down
 or anyone else I hold in my hand

Blood ink

Wide trunks and branches
cover mountainsides in growth
Sharp buzzsaws strip hope

Old wilderness trees
cry foul. Loggers yell *Timber!*
Forests bare till spring

Felled wood tied with chains
on trucks that weave to rivers
Walk/rolled fast to mills

Paper made from pulp
poured in vats, dyed in colors
Rife with arsenic

Blank journal pages
beg for life stories, sonnets
Soul's bark, louder, begs

Sonnrick I: To writers*

Once there was a writer from New Jersey
  published his cruel book posthumously.
Written when had enough, it sold galore,
  popular headlines brought memoir's high score.
The writer's spouse taken aback, mad, shocked,
  upset, fired up, husband's book not blocked.
Each page typed out by his bloody fingers,
  exposed her innermost feelings, each mocked.
    What hast thou done? she cried, permanent frown.
    Bared my soul, echoed ghost six feet _____.

The badgering wife swooned aghast, shaken,
  when heard coworkers, friends, cluck like chickens.
Caught in husband's raw confessions, had fits,
  'cause others said, *Her rep lies in the pits.*
But discount sales, wide acclaim, titles, fame,
  saved her skinny frame, home, car, prior name.
So dutiful wife forgave her bedside target,
  swallowed spouse's words with one regret:
    You told intimacies from our bed sack!
    Only expressed inner angst! Ghost shot _____.

Since King and widowed Queen of New Jersey
  survived decades of fights and outbursts,
the lesson for all to heed clearly and be:
  Tell truth honestly, hiding feelings hurts.
Persistence requires ev'ry writer,
  to share soul's heart to listening readers.
Still atop New York Times best seller list,
  Amazon royalties fill her open fist.
    Her mansion estate with gardeners, cars,
    makes all the taxmen much richer by ____.

* combination sonnet/limerick-like lines & sounds.

organic menthol

Santa Ana winds push Greyhound past Flagstaff, Amarillo
  warms my chilled bones in Northeast Trenton winters
thrills my chest after our IKEA memory foam trysts
  calms nerves when locked in County jail for robbery
clears head of diatribes against city hall potholes
  picks today's shortest crooked Waze to Philly
crosses streets and racing avenues in the Big Apple
  enjoys SiriusXM '60s and '70s channels and Beatle's
hum Fab Four's Magical Mystery Tour and Lady Madonna
  keeps me company in my third Honda Civic, car #14
upsets my wife, cardio doc, PCP, pulmonologist
  forks over sin taxes to New Jersey every morning
creates original haibuns and haikus in smoggy LA
  stops me, breathes in, exhales, in Central Park meditations
raises posters to show errors of Supreme Court jurists
  maintains forgotten Revolutionary War individualism
votes by mail for rare moderate independents
  releases arthritis in neck, jaw, fingers when yawn
compels yard chore mowing for July 4th cookouts
  watches Xavier win a cool 750k on BB23
eases pain now your alone in St. Mary's cemetery
  until I pass away

no one here anymore to care what ashes I leave
1960s sea glass ashtray, Dunkin' cup, jalapeno bagel
formaldehyde-free American Spirits, all with me
drawing me out of my future grave
  to put pen to page

_Toc1796 Error! Bookmark not defined.

      Damn eBook formats
      God, don't edit on the cheap
      Touchy Function Keys

Apolitical

Governing, conversations, opinions, even hat colors are political. This Age of Transition which started mid-1800s, is long and tortuous, loaded with minefields. Roses and hyacinths too.

Politicians, smoliticians, not everyone's perfect or does what we agree with. Too much diversity of opinion for that. I believe, most people are mostly good, will do the right thing, but some don't or won't for whatever their reason.

We can agree though, things could and should be better when it comes to politicians, politics, and governing.

Changes like term limits, multiparty representation, limits on campaign financing, business and government transparency, and greater participation by citizens in decisions will all occur. For every working U.S. employee, appointee, or official, mandatory retirement age will be set. The Electoral College—abolished. There'll be term limits and more.

These poems show a point of view, which we all have, and viewpoints change. So do poems. So do their crafters.

It's tough to govern imperfect humans when imperfect humans ourselves. Only spirituality and morals can extricate us from this mess we've established so far.

can't escape

calm on west coast as sun rises at LAX
but June's El Niño churns shore waves
    stirring, stirring
its due again, Americans know, but this,
different as people wake, start duties and chores
    feel breezes kick up in their faces
on the streets, hills, in front yards,
canyons, flats, windows, doors and
    saddleback mountain tops

winds push stronger by 9
dust storm pockets spin
    grow, enlarge, sprout dandelions
higher by 10
speed roils faster
    disturbed dust, dirt pushes, thickens
covers clear air and smog
one hundred feet then two
    drivers wipe windshields, sweat
clouds stay, move east, thicker
until Chicago reached

no one has an explanation
children, parents, seniors choke
    stay indoors or in vehicles, hibernate
its north-south sirocco wall, a thousand miles
wide, taller than towers, dwarfs old Sears
    fills crevices, bowers with prairie debris
shuts down air conditioning, electricity
emergency teams flounder, can't see
    chaos, fear, surprise, wringing of tears ensue
all enshrouded as sirocco moves, faster
over skyscrapers to the Atlantic's beaches
    FLA to ME, blinding, thick, thicker
heat from sea and dust lands 140 degrees

everything stops, nothing moves in any spot
   rooftops, lawns, streets, those in shelters
once running or standing water
covered by tons of clogging dirt, earth itself
   heavier than Caterpillars lift, break down
AC units universally closed, no help indoors
the sirocco halts
   the few left beg
please move off, Oh God, anywhere else
but it does not; it does not
   no one breathes
      not one has air
ever shifting, smothering political winds
   have murdered voters and children

blessed with two

we could have had one or
only two maybe three fingers
   with no opposable thumb
to twist open beer caps
drink from a cup
   hold knife and fork
insert flash drive
click mouse, see world pics.
   we use these hands, but
thousands go without
they carry on, troopers no doubt
   a hundred reasons for their loss but
accidents, disease, don't come first.
war, deadliest celebré of insanity
   hoisted upon us by heartless drones
loses capability to fully moan.
shout blame, point
   over loss of a face, leg, arm, hand, finger
that to me, is killing too

MIA again

realized it after large lopsided armies
tore into, occupied, annexed Crimea
provoked separatism, lied, called peaceful
Ukrainians the Nazi eff word
    hellbent Ruskies shelled, killed babies
    millions fled, broke families, had to run.
a year earlier Taliban took Afghan over
Americans fled, abandoned populace on tarmacs
    let stand harsh, cruel, Medieval ideology
nations yawned, kept arm and words extended
    what's excuse this time?
cry at human bondage, carnage, deaths—
avoidable with one firm unifed hand, but
Middle East not our land, won't shed
red-blooded Marines on foreign soil like Ukraine
Libya, Syria, Yemen, Sudan, Haiti when U.S. says *No*
    don't dare upset Jewish voters, Israel either
    best stretch only arm's length sympathy to Palestine

hear it whispered at private conference tables
    they're not rich white Europeans like us
we obfuscate their problems since not ours to fix, but
send Caterpillars, lay asphalt roads, span rivers
raise power plants, buildings, airfields, schools
part of our big buck business largesse
    reap billions for U.S. corporations pockets
    in Ike's feared military industrial complex

afraid of unstable dictator's threats
NATO won't bomb their bombers, killing jets
silos, bases, headquarters, too direct.
if begged and begged send weapons not men
    follow MAD's arm length deterrence
    obliterate false hope in hearts of oppressed

don't judge a book

by its cover sang bluesman Willie Dixon
cliche since 1860 heard ad finitum
surmise a struggling author first said it
maybe Poe, when his books didn't sell

it may be a crappy thing to ask when see
low ripped hanging jeans, purple mohawks too
on young guys going into Tiki bars to booze it
what the hell are they thinking?

and the explosion of tattooed arms
ankles, legs, buttocks, low backs, faces
suntanning at local muscle beaches
are they all Hells Angels or something?

my life's book cover disturbed staid elders
in '68, with shoulder-length hair, VW bus
white bell bottom tie-died jeans, leather sandals or
platform velvet shoes and knee-high sunburst daishiki

grown since the next decade heyday woke me up
forced to mature when two kids born
father/provider responsibilities emerged
stepped up to the plate, batted 250

cut my hair, took earring out
sold VW with curtains, bought a Corolla
fed my family, mortgaged a house
joined other second-class American Joes

however or whenever one judges another
appearances don't make the man, woman or youth
only what they do, say, not what they look like
should be used to send negative opinions out

I call them to account

mystery of mysteries, holy beyond holy
All-knowing, All-wise, only Thou sees
   if there's a future for American democracy
under thumbs of some lousy leaders
misogynists, crooks, despots, liars
insurgents, rebels, legal terrorists
economic battles for company supremacy
   our country burns, vanquishes liberties

now SCOTUS upturns social mores
sets back precedents from a hundred years
idealistic values, freedoms, scorned
who's worse, them or Presidents who chose
ultra-conservative deniers and naysayers
   of equal rights, fewer guns, impartial courts
I invoke Thy name at this human rights disloyalty
want equality, sanity, rationality to save civil polity
need your honest statesmen and women free to
voice wisdom, not attack, threaten, deny elections
   honest folk, without fear of reprisal, discredits,
   hammered, or excoriated by right-wingers

Oh God, Lord on high!
protect us from one-person appointees
let a strict bipartisan Commission vet, approve
who decides nation's rules, policies
   set mandatory retirement age at 80
term limits for elected officials
hold Constitutional Conventions, pass Amendments
   fix gaps, cement impartial justice, pay debts
no longer overlook donor sources and affiliations
PAC special interests, hurtful lying campaign millions
   Bring back fair in fairness
   Revive depressed spirits and hopes
   Make America great again and not just a slogan

Jabbingwhackies*

Twas thrilling as aisleways of slimy toads
Did fly and flutter twixt roll call gavels
Flimsy too these filibuster droners
As skedaddled back to Georgetown in droves

"Compare their slithery mocks to my girl Echo
Their teeth that tear, nails that scratch!
Beware their hard-shelled turtle skins, run,
Fear ultraconservative deceptions!"

She took uncle Hobbit's Sting in hand;
A foretime's awesome Smaug it fought
Cloaked invisible in dubloons and jewels
Under Capitol Dome's smashed rocks and bones

Deep in their scoffish laughs and schemes
Came ill-famed antichrist with heart of stone
Crawled sniffing from under ash-filled grandstands
Chortled put downs, curses as spouted lies

She skirts and dodges, my hero douses its attacks
As fears of stolen democracy surround peaceful Shire
My girl of righteousness spars, thrusts, parries
Till monster's toothy-pasted smile of hate tires

Stings of titanium "Zits!" "Zangs!" "Zings!"
Pierce it's thickset spiteful money grooves
Till, fallen from daughter's heroic onslaughts
It withers unto death, not bemoaned by smart citizens

Her father shrieks to media, kilk and kin
"Didst thou see my girl of elfish skin?
Defend our homes and breasts grown thin
O fab'lous Moons and Suns at highest!"

Pants-on-Fire Twitterer, the freedom killer died
Slain by fed up moderates with molten lead

Thrust thrice throughout each swollen head
Atop elitist Harvey Dent two-faced politician

Land of Shire equality returns to joviality
When all thought collegiality dead

*Parody of *Jabberwocky* by Lewis Carroll, part of my namesake

Some can't forgive

Pent-up intifada appalled, shook, shocked world eyes
Hamas massacre unleashed machetes, grenades
     slaughters, bullets, of murderous rage
     human bargaining chips hijacked, hidden
     felt sorry for Israeli music festival kids

In daily overkill native families displaced
abandoned, shot, blasted, buried under concrete
despite memories of SS propaganda lies
     more than six million Magen David stars
     arrested, imprisoned, gassed or starved
     yet genocide reigns again, again, again

Watch newscasts and flashes, videos, headlines, texts
red-painted blood-soaked campuses, street protests
confirm rock-hard slants for/against dual statehood
    this retired, coddled white American sympathizes
     but how could I, neither Jew nor Palestinian
     presume to feel Middle Easterners pain, anger?

Great Britain at First War's end, and U.N. resolution later
mandated Palestine's new borders instead of leaving it alone
Zionists seized land, made Arab-Muslims slaves with no voice,
dismissed their rights, built walls/fences, patrol, fire Uzis
     named it Israel of old although Judea expired
     while fanatical settlers inflame hate, sow rot

An ocean and sea away, see justified loathing in
brutal battles to regain or retain national sovereignty
      mothers' faces covered, streaked, stained
      sob, cry, wail, moan with battered hearts
    can't bring back siblings, husbands, parents, babies

Yahweh, Allah's, Names invoked don't halt 40,000 deaths
no wonder frustrated, bitter, disgusted with talks
since the Nakba, peace dashed, hope balked
      both factions profess one just, all-loving Lord but
      ceasefire holds no safe haven in this sea of war
where Land—once Holy—sank, disappeared

Dashed hopes seek relief, return of hostages
surcease from blood-soaked oppression
    no more dying every hour from fear, constant repression.
    ambassadors white paper truces offer no panacea
few admit truth: bygone eras can never be restored
      each side will be diaspora outcasts, no peace, not ever
unless adhere to Torah and Quran's law—*live together*

What someone did in West Bank, Gaza, Germany
Poland, Darfur, Rwanda, every spot, place, island
home to black, red, yellow, olive flesh, pink or brown
family, tribe, congregation, culture, nation
      can't, shouldn't, shall never be forgotten
      but must be forgiven to save innocents

Don't believe this lounge chair sympathizer
from America who plays only favorites in geopolitics
    heed your maimed and dead witnesses, victims
listen to your guiltless babes, boys, girls, women, men
beseech, plead, beg loudly through their white pine boxes
    This must not be allowed to continue. Stop it
If revenge endures no matter the righteous cause
    only scorched earth remains for hellfire graves
    no God will save their souls

Free speech hijacked

Jeff Bezos from Albuquerque converted Oscar Wilde's
Poems, essays into garage doors of pure internet gold
touted success for lowest prices, until Free Booksy
had to snigger over Penguin's & Border's losses
when POD and Kindles set publishing worlds on fire

Kafka broke his insect arm while dreaming in his bed
Roald Dahl's youthful James popped British questions tryin'
to tie complex rolling shoelaces with huge deadly peaches
Emily stuffed destitute Heathcliff's face with riches from
boxing bouts as jumped past Isabella's bed in one hop

J.K. Rowling's non-sexy blogs retold Dickens' stories
of youth lore troubles, compelled kids' gory attention in
a series of long dark robes and noses, Azkaban and surprised
authors who didn't ride Dementors and lost muggle readers

Mary Shelley mused mad in monster's tableau, alas poor
George Elliot's nom de plume watched, waited like an MI6
Bond operative, upped readers' confusion over Frankenstein and
Marlboro man knockoffs who sat in their silent saddles when tv
ads abolished so did black man Old Spice hit commercials

Twain's niggas first classic to go, Capote finds out mid-July
if too cold, typical lyric demonic storms appear in Rushdie's
Satanic guide as Bollywood scriptwriters slow burn like
spinning 45s shouting heretical words to fellow Muslims

King penned evil slingers, buried 50 hatchets in hotel doors
while Nabokov lit prurient bonfires under self-righteous feet
that erased Lolita's ink on pages for good when they
claimed intellectuals joined Communist Party communes

So goes intellectuals, books. Banned. Hated because extreme
politically correct persons afraid words will expose power in
truth, release new thoughts, questions, ideals, demands

each vote gold lamé

executive chiefs, legislators, hand-picked aides
pander sound bites to constituents, gullible voters
who hear, see, read regurgitated taglines to make
America in their great image, the one where
taxes low for the richer, abortion outlawed for
deathbed moms, walls, fences built to cut off legal paths
SWATs hired, disloyal ex-staff decimated

majority wins in November a huge coup
for red party platform, coffers too
seems like fear, crisis and division rules
no compromise, dismantle, gut Fed government too
ugly personal attacks means consensus chances slim

they repeat what high paid outside advisors proscribe
scriptwriters lay down rhetorical empty speeches
paid publicists send mass callouts for larger rallies
lukewarm responses mean second place polls, anathema
only fired up crowds generate the ire they feed on
despise opponents, bust columned domes, kill security

solution: make a big announcement
tell them all *You'll receive medals, honors*
tell them to *Show up in your best Armani suit*
for 6 o'clock Fox News cameras
drive them in fancy limos to RFK Stadium
lock doors, seal exits, at the signal detonate Semtex

the decent ones won't be harmed
didn't show up, too humble, wise
they seek majority's welfare, not theirs
reject special interest bribes, never pander donations
urge public toward free, fair civil laws, early voting
cut loopholes, tax millionaires, corporations
these deserve our praise, trust, hope, reelection

Another white rich demagogue

America has its share of manipulators
wrapped or warped ultra-powerful deal mongers
Egos toss aside ethical boundaries
   when hoodwinked electors hand over office

Every time has a place for bad actors
   The good defend themselves
   in the face of spurious, false accusations
   death-threat phone calls or hammers to the head

Such the case in 1950 congress
   an intelligence man from Wisconsin politics
His name Joe, communist and homosexual hunter
   his House committee destroyed reputations

Just like today, those who desecrate immigrants
   label them murderers, thieves, dog eaters, rapists
   built this country from strong backs since inception
2,000-mile walls impossible to hold back migration

Despots' common belief
   I know what's best
like kings of centuries past
false prophets today

crazed loyal followers
blinded by promised hyperbole
accept these wolves with blood-soaked fangs
in dyed white lie sharkskin coats

It's

It's my right! Fear me
Wage word swords against other-
wise normal people

E Pluribus Unum

Signers valued ideals, justice, freedom,
wanted enlightenment age for a free citizen nation.
Now their Constitution trampled
in hatred of other parties, misinterpretation

Declarations in '76 had high appeal,
made wealthy white Englishmen richer.
Gave unalienable rights to own guns and property,
juxtaposed free speech, religious tolerance

Life, liberty, and pursuits of colonial happiness
didn't free colored or immigrants from slavery.
But Abraham took a stance. Poor dead president.
Even democrats revere his selfless legacy

Articles of this old Charter impossible to amend today
but vitriol between party legislators bend it's precepts.
States, so fickle, won't ratify Equal Rights, open elections
want powers, prerogatives greater than federal

Can dig through Hamilton's grave and resurrect
Jefferson's Human Rights pen, Sally his example.
Only slim sliver of time remains to bring
Founders' goals into early 21st century

Stars and stripes hang by needle's thread
can't let black-booted politicians tread them to tatters.
Like I said, a few moments left to reconstitute
an all-inclusive flag to its true spiritual destiny

Everyone

Everyone hates war
except salaried soldiers
They keep peace as told

humans stupid they be

echoes TV's new baby Yoda, old Jedi Master
coddled, protected by face-helmeted Mandalorian.
condemnation of his truths seen in today's news
headlines, while fight bandits, robots, troopers too

eons before, honorable flags and names for nations
human tribes did what duplicitous politicians avoid—
joined their wills, governed justly, pooled resources,
trained minds, hands, backs, built friendly communities

cringe in this era, Fud disruptions, how we live
unfair laws or none where should, ruinous wars, factions
well-deserved unrest, extremists fundamentalism fatwas
violent campus protests and damn authorities who
serve secret special interests, beg campaign donations

the simplest solution, administer uniform fairness—
but rephrased clichés fail at solutions ad nauseum
they say *if only they/him/she/them would do it...* or
worse, the politician's *I have a plan, trust me.*
when they become King/Queen/Pope/President
weild their whims best in a blink of their eyelid

absolute power corrupts apple cores and spreads
unless hidden saint or benevolent prodigy appears
teaches humanity to unite universal Force for good
while devotees of chaos and martial law lengthen
pro-my-nation destructive courses with armies or
high-priced lawyers who deny a Lady Justice

it's men, always men. wheel/deal, wrest powerful posts
wealthy, influential, glib, bereft of empathy, decency
regardless of industry, but we employees rely on them
so stay mum, too big to fail or lock in jail, lose our jobs
time we called a spade a shovel and give me one
dig their grave and don't let them dig out

Will, jump in

as LA citizen over 35, file at city hall right now
name your independent party a status quo kicker
for a kid who lived in a Princely Bel-Air mansion
had a strong constitution from Philadelphian
Phanatic songs, hip hop movements that drew attention

your Hancock now invincible linked to Jadda
both versatile well-respected like Obamas
used to sound stages, a certified A-list actor
dancer, rapper, decisive hero in action movies
you topped Reagan and Bonzo's glory hours

you've won a hundred awards, three Oscars
proud family defender, slap offenders on stage
witty, charming, intelligent, winning smile
you've got my vote, allegiance, credit card and cash
go pound Tricky-Dick Manipulators into heaps of trash

we'll form an independent committee the IDRC
within hours sky's the limit dumped in campaign coffers
with your brand of family man, well-rounded demeanor
go now, now Mr. Smith, all the way to Washington's
Whitest House and past-meaningful monuments

we'll splash the good news on airwaves
give admirers wholesome solid concrete plans
show voters, world's nations, lost AMC moviegoers
we haven't forgotten
how Hollywood makes a man heroic

however, Mister President
don't let stinging words
provoke untrammeled fire
or push the red nuclear button higher

Contributors

Great thanks to friends, mentors, cohorts, and free spirits whom I learn from, read, see, and hear in my heart and soul. They simply and always awe me. Their works are available from any major bookstore in print, or their website, or online in print and eBooks

Virginia Watts

The author of poetry and stories found in *The MacGuffin, Epiphany, CRAFT, The Florida Review, Reed Magazine, Pithead Chapel, Sky Island Journal* et al. She's been nominated four times for a Pushcart Prize.

Her debut short story collection *Echoes from the Hocker House* was a finalist in the 2024 Eric Hoffer Book Awards, selected as one of the Best Indie Books of 2023 by Kirkus Book Reviews. It also won 3rd place in the 2024 Feathered Quill Book Awards. Ginny and I workshop poems weekly on Zoom with others. Please visit her at https://virginiawatts.com/

Michael P. Riccards, PhD

An educator, administrator, and three-time college president, Mike has written and published over 35 books of fiction, nonfiction, and plays, some produced on stage. At Hall Institute he wrote public policy essays. He's been a mentor and example to the Hamilton Creative Writers and now lives in Florida.

His autobiography, *A Hero in His Own Life*, and his *Grandpa* series of stories of wise advice, captivate hearts with vignettes of well-known people.

elliot m rubin

A 2024 Pulitzer Prize Entrant in Poetry for *Side Street Poems,* Elliot is a New Jersey poet who has authored and published over forty books of poems, and facilitates two Zoom poetry critique groups weekly.

Eliott's recent poetry books include *Banned beat Poems*, an Amazon bestseller at #2, and *Show Me the Bansky*, #4 on Amazon.

He has also published six crime novels, as well as poems in assorted anthologies, two with me and others. He lives in Central Jersey and loves the Shore (but not sand where it doesn't belong). Elliot has 12,000 poets follow him on Instagram at https://www.instagram.com/elliot_m_rubin/

Craig Sherman

I had the honor of editing Craig's first book, a novel/memoir titled *no good deed...* based loosely on his encounters as President of a synagogue. His work has appeared in online and print publications, including Poetica Magazine. He has contributed extensively as a blogger for the Huffington Post, and for a time hosted WDDF's classic rock radio program "Connections."

Craig received his undergraduate degree in Economics and Finance from Temple University where he worked at the literary magazine, The Journal of Modern Literature.

He earned his master's in management information systems from St. Peter's University, and his career in IT has spanned three decades.

Craig lives in NJ with his family and two rescue dogs.

Roberta Batorsky

A former cancer pharmacologist, she taught biology at Temple University in Philly and is a freelance science journalist besides poet and writer. She began her blog **solipsistssoiree/** in 2010 and is on Instagram too.

Roberta has lived in NJ for over 30 years, enjoys open mics, hiking, and spending time with her two grandchildren. For many years she has shared poems and stories at our weekly Creative Writers & Poets critique sessions at the Hamilton Public Library.

Jonathan Savrin

Jonathan writes insightful short stories, poems, and memoirs about unusual and stressful situations that are encountered during 'normal' life. After retiring from work as an environmental scientist with the New Jersey Department of Health, he honed his interest in creative writing skills by taking workshops at nearby universities and at local writing groups, including the Hamilton Writers & Poets for many years.

He has backpacked across Europe, spent time in Africa, and currently lives in Washington Crossing, PA.

Sienna Rose Richards

Granddaughter, writer, filmaker, artist, storyteller, reader, Lego master, our son calls her the most creative person he knows. A native New Yorker, she has a zest for smiles and action in her stories, with 2,500 subscribers on her YouTube channel, *Dayplay-siennarr*.

Her included poem *Grandad* was composed circa age 8. A collector too, like her Grandmum, she adores her Hazel Village friends. https://siennaroserichards.com/aboutme.php

Patricia Lebon Herb

A poet and painter in Middlebury, VT, her poems have been featured in *Vision and Verse* (ed. Les Bernstein 2024)*, Phases* (Redwood Writers 2023 Poetry Anthology), *Zig Zag Lit Mag*, *Borders in Globalization Review*, and the Swedish literary magazine *Provins*.

Patricia is of Belgian-Native American descent. lebonherbart.com

Joan Menapace is a visual artist and author of *The Mysterious Sister* (2023), a graphic novel, under the pen name Etoile Blanche, a chapbook, *Walking:* (2022) and has published works in *Poems from the Circle of Seven* (2023). She is currently working on a long narrative poem as a companion to her pantheon of feminine archetypes which can be viewed at www.joanmenapace.com.

Further info on her novel is at www.mysterygraphicnovel.com

She views poems as word collages. Putting words together to form an image for the reader, she believes, is much like selecting marks, colors and other media to create visual art. Her website is joanmenapace.com.

Donald Proffit

A former arts educator and school principal who has presented workshops, clinics, and original performances in Australia, Italy, Belgium, Canada, France, Israel.

Don and I met at a Princeton Library Authors fair. His book *Hardship Alaska* is a compelling memoir that weaves a young man's identity crisis with his conscience against the raw, transformative backdrops of 1970s Alaska.

The book has been shortlisted for the 2024 William Saroyan International Prize for Writing in the nonfiction category.

Marion Pollack

I first met Marion in a writing group circa 2013. Marion's work has been published in *Back in the Bronx, Kelsey Review* and *U.S. 1*. Her book *Grandma, Tell Us a Story, Tales of a daring hypochondriac* and her 2024 book of poems, *There's No Rush*, curls lips into smiles or guffaws with real-life daily adventures we can all picture clearly.

Her educational background includes a BS from Cortland College, and master's degrees from Northeastern University and The College of NJ.

She and husband Bob live in Lawrenceville, NJ, the house of desire in *There's No Rush*. They have two grown children and six grandchildren.

Robert M. Berry

Zero-(1955)-to Sixteen-(1970) in Valley View, Phillipsburg New Jersey in two story concrete house designed by Thomas Edison. Started playing electric bass at 14 at CBGB's to chamber music. Also play cello, piano and anything else I get my hands on that talks back.

Wrote my first poem in second grade: "I have a big Donkey I have a big Monkey – My Donkey is crazy - my Monkey is lazy." Apparently no one else could rhyme so I became a momentary hot shot.

Live near Philly PA. Build stuff, compose music, write poems, some acting and do "Fringy" live music and art stuff.

Sash Kalansuriya

Born in 1986, he dreampt of being a writer and a doctor both. He studied hard, graduating from Villanova University in 2008 with a Bachelor of Arts, then UMDNJ in 2012 with a Master of Biomedical Science, and then achieving his Medical Doctorate from Ross University in 2020.

Sash's broad interests inform his writing, as does reading. He doesn't stop doing either.

Sash has shared his work for years in Creative Writers & Poets sessions at the Hamilton Public Library and at the 2024 Authors Showcase.

William Waldorf

Bill's love affair with poetry began with strict forms like sonnets. Currently focused on poems from daily life, he loves to show history has not changed us. He continues to show romantic, touching, and mysterious sides of love in his latest poems, *Ways of Love,* Published by Prolific Pulse Press.

His previous book *Sonnets and More* explores various themes of love's relationships. His *Draw of love* was published by Ravens Quote Press.

Bill appears in several anthologies also, like *Poems from the Circle of Seven*, with me, Ginny, Joan, and Elliot et al.

TARA X

I don't know how to describe my
poems...
I just write
What I do know is that
creativity is a sign of being alive
Being alive is a blessing that
lasts for only now
There is only now
The lesson is a reminder that
every day is a better day
Make the most of it
There is health in creativity

Tara Chadha – London doctor,
poetess, actress, daughter, sister, aunt, friend, and lover. Tara is
published with me and others in *The Thursday Poets' Anthology.*

the author

I worked in the NJ Treasury Department
for 10 years in computer operations and
resource management, then spent 28
years as a certified purchasing agent and
contracts manager for statewide IT,
adding electricity and natural gas in 2002
until retired. I wrote and bid out the
State's first online reverse auction in
2006 for $100 million a year.

I've published eight books including
this and critiqued 5,000 pieces in multiple
weekly writing workshops since 2013, beginning poetry
composition a year later.

After retiring I taught business and technical writing to youth
for three years, and memoir writing to adults at Princeton Adult
School. I've written 270 topical Baha'i-themed essays published

on Bahai Teachings.org and contained in two volumes so far. 2021 saw a revamped publication of my bipolar memoir. In 2024 I collaborated on two volumes about starting, running, and growing any type of small services business.

Through my company ABLiA Media, I've edited my work and 30 memoirs, novels, poetry, short stories, and published 15 for clients available on Amazon. This is my first book of vetted poems, and I truly thank its contributors and friends.

I'm an active follower of Baha'u'llah, founder of the worldwide Baha'i Faith. In my locality, I've served as a volunteer court dispute resolution mediator for 24 years. I served on the Environmental Advisory Commission for seven, helping to establish a Green Team and an environmental award program. I'm a volunteer at my town's public library as part of The Friends of the Hamilton Library, since 1984.

Married a longtime, as you well know by now, with two incredible adult children and delicious grandchildren.

Caio and best wishes

Rod

PS I apologize if this is too male centric. As stated, males and females are equal. Each contains elements and qualities of the other.

Acknowledgments

My wife Janet puts me to shame.

We met in high school in 1967 and remain together whether rollercoaster adventure or calm seas. She put herself through college, became a teacher, and taught 3,000 elementary students for almost 3 decades until retiring. The next 10 years she was an adjunct instructor at Rider University certifying new teachers, a private professional development presenter and consultant, and an online writing tutor for banned Baha'i college students in Iran.

For 30 years she edited the Central Jersey Baha'i newsletter and has been chair, treasurer, and secretary of our local Baha'i council. She served as treasurer of the Mid-Atlantic Region Association of Baha'i Studies for many years, among many other posts and positions. Creative and active, she established McGruff House for latchkey kids, a book club, and co-founded The Friends of the Hamilton Public Library in 1984.

Our son Jesse and daughter Kate make us incredibly proud and happy parents and grandparents.

and...

My son Jesse. Artist/designer/guru, published author, family man, and Manhattanite for life. His first book, *The Secret Peace*, and Janet inspired me to write my first book.

Hamilton Creative Writers & Poets. Since 2013, they help me hone my craft. Shout out to Hamilton Public Library Director Scott Chianese who lets us host in-person sessions there weekly.

Sunday Poets Zoom poetry group led by Bill Waldorf.

Edgar Allan Poe. An inspiration and influence, along with Byron, Billy Collins, Ray Bradbury, and Terry Goodkind.

Baha'i friendships. They keep any spirituality I have alive.

Music and books. Ladders to wings that soar my soul.

Contact

Contact me at **1950ablia@gmail.com**

Please include the subject and your email address. Or contact me for editing, polishing, formatting, and publishing services through my website https://rodneyrichards.info/

Thanks for reading!

I'd be grateful if you'd post a review on Amazon or other venue of your feelings and thoughts on the content or issues brought up in this book. Your interest makes a difference. I read all reviews so I can appreciate your feedback and respond when practical.

Find me on Facebook at **rodneywriter** or on Instagram at **rrichardswriter.** Check out my blog for writers at **https://writewithauthority.blogspot.com/**

Thanks for your support!

Rod

PS Write your stories and poems! I hope to read them. It's never been easier to self-publish or hybrid-publish for next to zero or little cost. I recommend Amazon KDP and Draft2Digital.

My books/eBooks on Amazon.com & elsewhere:
Solving the World's Titanic Struggles, two volumes (2018 & 2022), 100 essays each, published by ABLiA Media LLC
Coffee, Cigarettes, Death & Mania (2021), memoir 275 pp., published by ABLiA Media LLC
Chester says Be Your Own Boss, two volumes (2024), Starting, running, and growing a small services business, published by ABLiA Media LLC, with George I. Martin, EdD
Poetry Anthologies, Rod & others, published by ABLiA Media LLC: *The Thursday Poets' Anthology* (2022), and *Poems from the Circle of Seven* (2023)
Episodes, my first memoir, is out of print

Why Baha'i?

The Baha'i Faith was beyond obscure when I first heard of it in 1969. I lived in a shared-rent, six-bedroom home in the well-to-do West End of Trenton, NJ. The house was so big, we played tennis against the walls of our dining room, had a library with pocket doors, a back stairway from the kitchen to the 2nd floor, a surrounding porch, and Tommy's '63 Jaguar engine in the basement.

Drugs and alcohol flowed from our regular pusher, Charlie, who visited often with free junk. Two of the guys and Margaret were in Trenton State College. Two other guys worked. I spoon-fed meals to geriatric patients at Trenton Psychiatric Hospital. It was hippie time, party time, college and beat the draft time.

I was soaking it all in.

One evening a guy named Ted stopped over to see one of the guys, but they weren't there. I led him into the library and stayed to be polite. We started talking and he mentioned Baha'i.

Instantly attracted and curious, I peppered questions until Janet came over for our date. She happened to know Teddy as an ex-classmate, so she sat and listened too, interested.

Truth can only be discovered when open to it.

The rest is our history. Jan and I attended talks called firesides at homes of area Baha'is, meeting many. During months of inquiry, they gave us books and pamphlets to read, even personal prayer books. We traveled to events around the state, bought more books, and met tons of folks at places like the Teaneck Baha'i Cabin. The people were normal, kind, and loving.

In July 1970, we both joined. We found truth in an odd, unexpected, surprising way, didn't even know we were searching, and have been happy and grateful since.

In June '71 we married. But you know all of this and more from my poems. If you find of this interest and want more, you can pick up my memoir, essays, or other poems.

Thanks for being such good readers and listeners.

INFORMATION ON THE BAHÁ'Í FAITH

The Faith teaches unity, oneness, peace, cooperation, and love for every human being and God. It is the same spirit contained in the scriptures of all of God's holy messengers, updated for each age in which They appear.

'Abdu'l-Bahá, Bahá'u'lláh's Son, said this about what it means to be a Bahá'í: "...be the embodiment of all human perfections."

Contact Information: 1-800-22-UNITE (800-228-6483)

U.S. Baha'i website https://www.bahai.us/

Bahá'í World website https://www.bahai.org/

Find Baha'i quotations at https://www.bahai.org/library/

www.bahaiteachings.org contains essays on current topics by varied writers, including mine.

Fini

Diogenes of Sinope (c.404-323 BC) is known for saying, "I'm searching for an honest man" while walking around with a lamp in broad daylight. Siddhartha knew it was within oneself.

Made in the USA
Columbia, SC
09 November 2024

45179446R00085